# GRAVEYARD SOCIETY

## BOOK 3

## This Was Your Life

EVERETT D WAIR SR

PAGE PUBLISHING
Conneaut Lake, PA

First originally published by Page Publishing 2024

ISBN 979-8-89157-359-8 (pbk)
ISBN 979-8-89157-405-2 (digital)

Printed in the United States of America

In Loving memory of my mother, Marie Wair

# INTRODUCTION

Welcome back to another *Graveyard Society* story: *This Was Your Life.*

This story is about a young man who has wondered for years why his half sister and brother hated his mother and why his own father hated him. It wasn't until his death that his soul was able to confront his sister and explain what really happened to them when they were little kids. He had to set the record straight so he could rest in peace.

# CHAPTER 1



*October 30, 1985*

Here I am, Creadel Jones, on the worst day of my life, standing at the gravesite of my mom, Marie Jones, on this cold, dreary, cloudy, rainy day. The funeral service for my mother here in Restvale Cemetery on the far south side of Chicago is in process. Many friends of my mother along with a few family members are in attendance. I stand there at my mother's grave as she's being lowered into the ground. I look at her stepdaughter, Glodious Jones, and stepson, Travon Jones, wondering what they are really thinking about my mother, what they are really feeling and saying in their minds about the woman their father asked to help him raise another woman's bastard kids. I am the oldest of the three. My mind drifts back to the time I first met them both. The year was 1956.

*1956*
*St. Louis, Missouri*

I remember that night my father, Vaughn Jones, and one of his brothers Richard Jones and I went to get them from their biological mother. I remember it so well, as clear as day, because it was that night my little ass was cold as an iced cube. We trod down the middle of a St. Louis street in the midst of a blizzard.

Even though I was a little dark chocolate-skinned boy, Vaughn dressed me warm in my white long johns, thick socks, long-sleeved T-shirt, thick hoody, blue jeans, snow boots, snow gloves, and a cap with earflap to keep my ears warm. But my face and nose were colder than an iceberg.

My pops, Vaughn, a dark-complexioned man in his late thirties, was wearing a black suit with the pants' cuff tucked deep inside his snow boots. His winter coat was a navy-blue peacoat. His leather gloves kept his hands warm, but the snow piled on top of his head must have felt like a large iceberg on his head, and his brother Richard Jones—also in his thirties, dark complexion, a salt-and-pepper beard, short Afro—wore two black hoodies, blue jeans, and a black leather that was popular in those days. He always wore this wide-brimmed, black, Smokey-the-Bear-looking type hat all the time.

We came to the middle of a block and turned down a dark alley to a five-foot wooden fence with a wooden gate that was partially stuck open from a mound of hardened snow.

Pop kicked open the wooden gate even further with his foot. We went inside the backyard of a house with a rear bedroom at the back of it. A side outer door that was connected directly to that bedroom was locked. My pop kicked open the bedroom door. *Bam!* We went inside. We saw several little kids lying in a single bed in this very, very hot bedroom. The little toddlers were all asleep.

Rushing, Pop quickly wrapped his illegitimate daughter, Glodious, in a blanket, and his brother grabbed my illegitimate half brother, Travis, in his toddler T-shirt and diaper and wrapped him in another blanket lying on a nearby chair. The three of us with the two toddlers rushed out the bedroom door leading back into the alley and disappeared into the cold, snowy blizzard of the night. They were too young to realize what was happening to them that night.

My father took these kids to my Aunt Nazzalee's apartment where my mom was. This was the first time my mother ever laid eyes on the two little adorable toddlers. Mom opened the front door to the blizzard swiping windy snow behind us and saw us standing. Pop had a sad look on his face. Mom's eyes dropped to the two little kids standing in front of him. She looked puzzled. Pop asked her to help him.

"I need your help," he said to her.

Stunned, she opened the door, and we entered the apartment.

I remember that his request was very disturbing to her because she didn't even know he had been having an affair and had been unfaithful. Of course, she was hurt, as any married woman would be. She didn't know what to do about these two little toddlers in her presence. I stared at them both curiously as we all gathered in the living room of the apartment.

"Who are these kids?" I asked myself.

"I don't want them staying with us," I remember saying to my mother.

As a little child myself, I felt that my little world was being invaded, and I just wanted my mom and pop. Of course, at that very young age, I didn't realize what I was saying and didn't really mean it. It just came out that way. I didn't understand what was going on. I was afraid and confused.

After my mother talked to some of the female family members, she decided to help him raise these two kids. Some women would never accept another woman's kids to raise, kids she didn't have a clue existed until he brought them to her.

It didn't take long for me to love them unconditionally and accept them as my brother and sister. I had always wanted a brother and sister, but God only blessed my mom with only me. We had some great years growing up. My mom did the best she could for them even though Pops was hardly around to help her, too busy chasing other women, fraternizing and being a policy runner in the numbers racket (otherwise known as policy racket).

We grew up, had our own kids, got married, partied, and lived a good happy life even after Mom passed away in 1985. Few years later then, Pop passed.

I thought we were happy siblings during those years that followed. I was very much mistaken. I realized in my vintage years that things wasn't really what it seemed with my half sister. All those years in the past of us growing up, I didn't know or realize that my sister had been holding something deep inside her. I didn't know that she was holding an ill will, an angry grudge inside her for years against the woman her father asked to raise her, my mother. She kept it to herself until she got older in her twenties. She hated my mother with a passion I never saw in her when I was around her and her brother. She blamed my mother for them being taken away from their mother. Nothing could be further from the truth. She gave my mother a very rough time every chance she got during the years of Mom raising them. I was living in Wichita, Kansas, at the time. I was not aware of this situation until I got a call from my cousin Ruth who was living across town from my mother, telling me that I needed to go to Chicago and see about my mother, that the two siblings were doing things to her.

All these years of loving these two siblings, thinking that they felt the same about me, man, I was so wrong. But I must say, my half brother told me that he apologized to my mom before she passed away, and I'm good with that. We remain close to this day.

But, on the other hand, my half sister hated my mother. And all my mother got in return was abuse and harassment, and she even attempted to kill my mother by putting small pieces of broken glass in my mother's food on her plate, hoping that my mom would bleed to death inside and die.

*Present Day*

It's a sunny day along Chicago's beautiful Lakefront. Joggers are jogging along the bike path with their dogs on. The lake's waves crash the shores into many huge gray boulders that line the banks. People are walking on the jagged huge boulders along the shore of Chicago's Lake Michigan. I have even seen couples trying to hid among the boulders, having sex. LOL. Imagine seeing that on a sunny hot summer day.

About twenty miles away to the west of the lake is Cook County Hospital, an old landmark structure on the west side of Chicago. An ambulance makes it way to the emergency room driveway entrance. The paramedics hop out and quickly open the rear door of the ambulance. On a gurney is a Black male teenager with very badly burned, bloody, and blistered face being pulled out and rushed inside. The emergency room is crowded with the sick and injured waiting to be seen.

In the emergency waiting room, an African American woman in her thirties is holding her crying one-year-old son. The woman stares at that the paramedics rushing past her with the burned teenager on the gurney. Doctors and nurses rush to the aid of the burned victim on the gurney. A man in his forties, Caucasian, and in business attire vomits onto the floor. An Asian lady of the night is dressed in a black miniskirt, a pink wig with bangs, with the rest of the hair resting on her shoulder, and a pink blouse showing a little cleavage. She has a tattoo of two naked women intertwined on her left upper arm. She pops her gum and stares at the Caucasian man who just vomited on the floor.

"Ooo…gross," says the Asian lady of the night.

On the second floor of the hospital, in the ICU room, is a seventy-five-year-old African American man named Creadel Jones. Creadel is on life support. An IV is inserted in his left arm. He's hooked up to a heart monitor. His body lays underneath the white sheets. His eyes are closed as he seems to be barely breathing. His room has a mounted TV hanging on the wall in front of his bed. There is a chair by the window. A flower arrangement sits in the middle of the bedroom window. Creadel has a salt-and-pepper beard, bald head, mustache, dark complexion, and tattoo of a scorpion on his left arm.

Standing at the foot of his bed is a transparent entity: a transparent woman in her forties, Caucasian, has long blond hair, has white rimmed glasses, and dressed in an all-white gown. She just stands there, staring at Creadel, saying nothing. A nurse, Asian, in her thirties, enters the room and starts checking Creadel's vitals and looks at his chart on the clipboard hanging at the end of his bed. She can't see the spirit woman standing at the end of Creadel's bed, watching her. The nurse grabs a tissue napkin from the box lying on the table next to the monitor and wipes Creadel's forehead. She checks off a few things on his clipboard and leaves the room.

Outside, over Lake Michigan, large light and dark-gray clouds begin to form with streaks of lightning. There are sounds of thunder as the cloud slowly grows and approach the hospital.

The spirit lady in white walks to the side of Creadel's bed and stares down at Creadel Jones.

"It's time, Creadel. It's time for your journey," says the spirit lady in white.

The heart monitor flatlines. Alarms send a team of doctors and nurses running into the room and trying to revive Creadel back to life, but to no avail. Creadel's life was no more. None of them can see the spirit lady in white in the room standing at his bedside. His body is covered with the white sheet, and they all leave the room.

The spirit lady stares down at Creadel's corpse on the bed. Using her mind, the sheet covering Creadel's body begins to pull down his body to the foot of the bed.

"Creadel," she calls out to him. "Rise, Creadel Jones."

She patiently waits. The soul of Creadel Jones rises from his body and sits on the side of his bed. He looks around the room, then back down at his corpse lying like a cold-ass, stiff-dead zombie on a hard-ass bed.

"I'm dead?"

"As dead as you can be," says the spirit lady in white.

He stares down at his lifeless body, then at the woman standing and waiting with her hand out to him.

"Who are you?" Creadel asks.

"I'm the spirit known as ghost MaGillicuddy."

"MaGill…what? Who?" asks Creadel.

"I know it's difficult to pronounce, but we have to leave now. It's time."

"Where? And the hell? Oops, I shouldn't use that word," says Creadel. "Am I going down there to…you know, that other place, below?" asks Creadel.

"I'm not at liberty to say," says the ghost lady in white.

Creadel takes her hand, and the two of them walk through the wall of his hospital room and vanish.

Two weeks later.

# CHAPTER 2

A southside funeral is in process. Creadel's body lies in a room with lots of funeral arrangements around his gray coffin. A few visitors drift inside and view his body. He looks so made up, dead and stiff in his black suit, white shirt, and black tie.

A dark-complexioned African American woman, Glodious Jones, now in her fifties, dressed in a black skirt with matching blazer, stockings, and shoes and has a black, wide-brimmed hat with an artificial rose on its side is Creadel's half sister. Yes, the woman whom his mother raised when she was a little child.

Glodious walks slowly down the long aisle separating the twelve rows of long seats, with only a few people sitting in both sections. Another observer, a lady standing at the coffin, stares at Creadel's body and wipes the tears from her eyes with a white handkerchief and leaves. Glodious walks to Creadel's coffin and stares down at his stiff-looking face.

"Well…I'll be—" Creadel's voice says in his dead mind. "I didn't think she cared enough to even come and pay respect to me."

"I'm glad your ass is dead, Creadel, along with your fucking mother. I ain't ever liked you anyway," says Glodious in her mind.

"You…came to my funeral…stand at my coffin…and say some stupid-ass shit to my dead-ass body this way!" Creadel says in his thoughts. "Don't you know you're talkin' to the dead, fool? I may be dead as all hell…but the dead can still hear your ass. R-E-S-P-E-C-T," says Creadel.

"I hope you rot in hell," says Glodious in her mind as she wipes away fake tears. "Can you hear my thoughts, dead man?" asks Glodious.

"Oh…you have no…idea. I definitely hear your ass, Glodious. You're lucky I'm dead, because if I wasn't, I'd have to see what the hell is your problem."

"You know, Creadel, I always pretended to like your ass as a sister. But, in fact, I really hated your mother more. Too bad, she didn't die from the bits of pieces of glass I put in her food back then," says Glodious in her thoughts.

As Glodious walks away from the coffin, the coffin starts to shake and tremble so bad that it falls over onto the floor. Creadel's body hangs halfway out of it, his eyes open, staring at Glodious. Glodious, frightened, rushes out the funeral home.

"Ain't that a bitch," says Creadel.

*Oak Wood Cemetery*

A funeral procession is making its way to a freshly dug grave in Oak Wood Cemetery. The procession stops a few yards from Creadel's grave. The funeral hearse stops. The hearse's rear door is opened and six pallbearers pull Creadel's coffin out. They place his coffin on their shoulders and start doing a traditional Ghana dance called Coffin Dance.

"The idea is to provide the deceased with a flamboyant and upbeat send-off instead of a solemn ceremony. But, before proceeding with the performance, the pallbearers will still have to ask the bereaved family if they want to give their loved one a traditional funeral or a 'dancing trip' to heaven."

The soul of Creadel and the lady in white are standing at a distance, watching the procession and the pallbearers dancing their way toward Creadel's gravesite.

The procession passes through mausoleums and headstones with arrangements placed over graves in the cemetery until they come to a stop at Creadel's open grave. Two gravedigger wait behind the people attending the service at a distance with shovels in hand.

"Since I'm dead and a ghost, you must be an angel or something," says Creadel.

"I'm whoever you want me to be," says the spirit lady in white.

"Oh, really? Okay then." Creadel thinks of the woman as someone he knew when he was alive. "Um, okay, my friend Ms. Muchenface Rawlins, can you be her?" asks Creadel.

The spirit lady in white changes into the image of a very attractive, sexy-looking, exotic African American woman named Muchenface Rawlins.

"Um…be…Cleopatra," commands Creadel.

She changes into the Egyptian woman Cleopatra and starts doing an Egyptian dance.

"Wow," says Creadel.

"Here's one for yah. What about that clown in Stephen King's movie?"

"You mean the clown with the last name Wise…or something like that?"

"Yep," says Creadel.

She changes into Pennywise, the clown, and stares into Creadel's eyes with its hideous stare.

"Oh shit, you're scary as hell."

"I'm just a spirit that brought you to your resting plot here in Oak Wood Cemetery," says the spirit lady in white.

Creadel stares at his headstone with his name and years on it. "Damn, not many people here for me," says Creadel.

"You are still loved by God," says the spirit lady in white.

"Well…thank you for enlightening me."

The pastor says a few words and a prayer over his grave. Creadel watches his gray coffin being lowered into the ground. He looks depressed and saddened.

"It's going to be okay," says the spirit lady in white.

"So you say," replies Creadel.

The pastor walks back to his car to leave, and all the vehicle leaves out the cemetery's huge green steel gate at the entrance. Creadel's grave is covered with the earth's graveyard soil. The spirit lady in white has disappeared. Creadel, standing alone, scans the graveyard, looking for her. He stares back down at his grave.

"Well…ashes to ashes…dust to dust…my Black ass has hushed its fuss. Amen," says Creadel. "I don't know what the hell I'm thinking. I don't even know how I feel being dead and all."

He sits on top of his covered grave with his back against his headstone. His head drops in sadness.

# CHAPTER 3

It's 2:00 a.m. in Oak Wood Cemetery. The graveyard is quiet, and the moon is full. Only a few clouds are passing in the night sky slowly. The cemetery starts to transform into its nightly appearance of a society of ghostly activities. Ghosts from various time periods are beginning to rise from their graves and come out of their mausoleums. Neon signs over the transparent business entrances doorways of various mausoleums (Barbershop, Grave's Cinema, Police Station, Voodoo Store, Bowling Alley, Graveyard Society Community Civil Hall, and even an All-Ghosts Baptist Church) start to come alive and become active. Ghosts' chorus, singing inside the church.

Off in the distance, at the opposite end of Oak Wood Cemetery, the graveyard grounds begin to shake and rumble with streams of smoke rising from beneath the grounds of a large open area in the graveyard. Suddenly, a huge, beautiful, transparent carousel rises.

A clown resembling Pennywise is preparing his cotton-candy machine for all ghosts and kids to enjoy the fluffy-tasting candy. The sound of carnival music is heard coming from an old, grand, long pipe organ. A transparent male ghost from the 1960s—Caucasian, dead, cold gray, wrinkly skin with a few strands of hair, rotten suit, shoes, shirt, with a rotten hole in his wide-brimmed hat—is popping popcorn at his popcorn machine. A woman ghost, dressed in ballerina attire, is injecting air into her many different-colored balloons with an air machine and tying them on a pole. A large tent has game machines for ghosts kids to play and win prizes.

A huge tent with a stage in front of it has large banners of images of Franceso Lentini—the three-legged man—on both sides of the stage. An old-style, 1940s microphone is at the center of the stage. The showman announcer—a transparent, midget male ghost with a disfigured half face and big top hat, dressed in a rotten coat with a tail, an oversize clown, black shoes, a bloodstained, rotten white shirt, and dirty white gloves—steps to the tall microphone that he has to tilt it over to speak into it. Instrumental music by the singing group Blue Magic's "Sideshow" starts playing. The showman announcer starts singing the lyrics to the music.

"Hurry…hurry…step right up. See the saddest show in Oak Wood Cemetery for only fifty cents. Step right up before the show begins. My friend, stand in line…get your tickets. I hope you will attend. It'll only cost you fifty cents to see…what life has done to you and me. See, that man with the broken feet is sad…he hurts so bad. There's got to be no sadder show to see…no doubt about it… satisfaction guaranteed," the showman sings out into the cemetery. He stares out into the graveyard, looking for ghosts to arrive. He looks at the three-legged man onstage behind him. "He has three legs and feet!" he tells the cemetery of ghost. "Costs only fifty cents to… attend! Hurry! Hurry!"

Lots of ghosts have risen from their graves and come out of mausoleums and start walking down the graveyard asphalt paved roads toward the carnival. Ghost kids are happily playing as they go down the graveyard asphalt road of Deadcold Avenue toward the carnival. Ghosts from various time periods are strolling through the graveyard to the carnival.

Not far from Creadel's grave is another mausoleum. Its door entrance begins to illuminate and pulsate with a lime-greenish color around the edges. Above the door reads the name Lil Candy residency.

Her mausoleum's dark-gray door stops glowing. The door slowly opens, and the face of Lil Candy—a forty-five-year-old, gorgeous transparent woman, African American, dead-gray complexion, with perfect makeup, long eyelashes, red lipstick, rouge, and long blond hair in a ponytail—peeks out the doorway. She's the spitting image of Lena Horne. Lil Candy sees several ghosts passing in front of her residency, going toward the carnival.

"Oh, boy, the carnival is here. I'm going to have some serious fun," says Lil Candy.

She steps out of her mausoleum, showing her sexy, shapely body and sexy legs, wearing a red miniskirt, white blouse with buttons just below the center of her breast, and red high heels on her sexy legs that's wearing fishnet stockings. Her fingers are well-manicured with red matching nail polish to match her miniskirt. A red shoulder purse with a gold chain is hanging on her shoulder. She pulls out a pack of cigarettes and lights one, staring around the graveyard as she lights her cigarette and blows out the smoke. She starts walking down the cemetery's asphalt road toward the carnival.

The graveyard is illuminated from the full moon. Off in the distance, the carnival's lights brightens the sky above it. The sexy legs of Lil Candy are slowly strolling down the center of the graveyard road with mausoleums on both sides with headstones in between them. She stops her stroll instantly when she sees the name of Creadel Jones on a headstone and him lying on top of his grave like a stiff corpse.

*It can't be*, she thinks. She steps closer to get a better look. "Creadel…Jones?" she says to herself. "No…can't be."

Her memory comes into her mind of them when they were kids in a house and hiding behind a big wide leather recliner. "That is his ass," she says with a frown on her face. "Wake up!" She kicks his feet. "Wake up, you teenie…weenie…dick motherfucker!"

Creadel wakes up, stunned, stretches, rubs his eyes, and focuses on the diva standing over him. "Why the fuck…are you kicking me for, lady?"

"You don't know me?" asks Lil Candy.

"Can't say that I do. Should I?"

"Take a good…look at this face," says Lil Candy.

"Lady, I have never seen you before in my life and definitely not in my death," says Creadel.

"Really!" Lil Candy stoops down closer to Creadel's face. "Take a good…look at these lips, dude."

Creadel stares at her lips. "Pretty lipstick," he says.

Lil Candy shrugs.

Creadel stands up. "Look, sista, you have me mistaken with someone else, you feelin' me?"

"Oh…yes…I have felt you. You just don't remember when I felt you, but don't worry, you'll come around." She puffs on her cigarette with her hand on her hip. "You just arriving here?" she asks.

"You can say that," replies Creadel.

"So you haven't had a chance to get used to the place yet?" asks Lil Candy.

"Naw. I haven't thought much about this whole dead thing yet, being dead and all," says Creadel.

"You want a smoke?" asks Lil Candy.

"I don't smoke."

"More for me," says Lil Candy. She looks him over. "You know, you look better than I thought you would after all these years," she says, looking down at his groin area. "Not too shabby…at all. You want to go with me to the carnival down there?" she asks.

He looks in the direction of the carnival. "Yeah, sure, why not?"

"Good, maybe on the way, I can refresh your memory or something and welcome you to our graveyard society," says Lil Candy.

They walk down the asphalt paved road in the cemetery toward the carnival.

"So you just got here, Creadel?"

"You asked me that already. Yeah, 'bout a week ago," he replies.

"Well, let me show you a few things here in Oak Wood Cemetery's graveyard society," Lil Candy says. "You see that mausoleum over there (*pointing*)?" asks Lil Candy.

"Yeah," replies Creadel.

"That's Gravestone Production Studio where they produce ghost movies…ghost thriller…ghost triple X-rated movies…and other ghosts stuff. You get the picture, don't cha?" says Lil Candy.

"Oh yeah, I think," says Creadel.

"As a matter of fact, I am going there for a production shooting tomorrow. You want to come with me?"

"Naw," says Creadel.

"Why not! You ain't got anything else to do but rest in peace from now. Come on…and go with me. You just might like it, Creadel. They're shooting an episode of *This Was Your Life* tomorrow. Let's bond…spend some time together. Don't look like you ain't interested in going. That's the least you can do after all these years. You need to pick up where you left off when we were young," says Lil Candy.

"You keep saying stuff about us knowing each other when we were kids, and for the death of me, I don't have a freakin' death's clue of what you're talking about."

"That mausoleum to the right of you is the cemetery's theater, and down there is the graveyard's courthouse mausoleum where ghosts stand trial for high crimes, sex offenders, and misdemeanors. And that one over there is the graveyard's society club."

"Really?" says Creadel.

"There's even a police station to hold ghost criminals in lockup. You know…if you think of something or wish it, it can possibly happen here in this society of ghost," says Lil Candy.

"Wow, this place is something, all right," says Creadel.

"Now, back to us," says Lil Candy.

"There is…no us," replies Creadel.

Lil Candy stops dead in her tracks, puts her hands on her hips, and stares into his eyes. "Look here, CJ. It just takes a minute. Dig deep back in your mind to when we were kids living in Little Rock, Arkansas. We were two kids at somebody's house…me and you went into, I guess, was the large room all…by…ourselves…and you wanted me…to suck your little weenie…behind a big-ass large… leather recliner where nobody could see us. Lord…help me. I was so naive back then as an innocent and defenseless and helpless little cute girl…but…you…wanted me to suck on your little johnny man. And I sucked it like nobody's business…even though it was absolutely my first time. You remember that, CJ?"

"I never!" yells Creadel.

"Oh, like hell you did…and I did it," says Lil Candy.

"I was a little weak at the knees back then." She takes a sigh. "I didn't know what I was doing…I wasn't even fully developed, too young. I couldn't even get Johnny man to rise to the occasion," says Creadel.

"You tellin' me," says Lil Candy.

"So stupid of me," says Creadel. "Well, you acted like you knew how to play house," says Creadel.

"You thought me…well…it was trial and error," says Lil Candy. "And you know what? I've been playing house ever since," says Lil Candy.

"I-I-I'm so…sorry, Lil Candy," says Creadel bashfully.

"I ain't got no regrets, baby. You turned me into a good…weenie's sucker."

Creadel is thinking. "I remember you now. You were that little girl way back then?"

"Yep, that was me."

"That was the only and last time I saw you," says Creadel.

"I have always wondered what happened to you as years pass," says Lil Candy. "Well, now we've been reunited in death," says Lil Candy.

"Yeah, I guess you're right. Hell, you are looking kinda fine…as hell for a ghost," says Creadel.

"You ain't so bad yourself."

"Well, at least, I have a friend here in this graveyard," says Creadel.

"Shit…we're gonna have a good thing while we're here, and let's start with the carnival," says Lil Candy.

"Sounds good to me," replies Creadel. "You know, you have a good-ass memory," says Creadel.

Lil Candy takes Creadel's hand, and they continue their walk to the carnival and have fun the rest of the night, riding the Ferris wheel, riding the roller coaster, playing carnival games and winning prizes, eating cotton candy, etc.

# CHAPTER 4

It's four o'clock in the morning, and the carnival is shutting down. Ghosts are leaving, some retreating back into their graves, others inside their mausoleums. Lil Candy is eating from a bag of popcorn as she and Creadel walk back down the cemetery's dark paved road.

"Man, I had a good time tonight," says Lil Candy.

"Yeah, same here."

The cemetery is still illuminated from the full moon, and they see two male transparent ghosts: Mr. Dexter who has a decomposed body skin, is in his eighties, is an African American, has long gray beard, is wearing a rotten white shirt with rotten holes in it, has a head that's partially bald with gray strands of hair, has a mustache, has a bifocal wire framed glasses with a cracked lens resting on his nose, and has rotten shoes as he sits across from a round tree stump with dominos on it in front of his friend Mr. Jed, a Caucasian man of the same age as Mr. Dexter. His transparent body is also decomposed. His hair is gone; his face is sunken on his jaws and eye sockets. He has a long grey mustache and beard. His rotten overalls are dirty, with holes, along with his rotten black T-shirt. He sits across from Mr. Dexter, holding dominos, contemplating on which domino to lay down.

At the entrance of Mr. Dexter's mausoleum is an old, dirty, analog TV with antennas bent over and cobwebs hanging off them. The TV cord has a cut-off end as it lays on the mausoleum steps on the side of the TV. The screen on it is statical and snowy but still able to see the 2020 Republican National Committee with Donald Trump speaking at the podium.

Mr. Dexter slams a domino down hard on the tree stump. "Give me five!" he yells out.

"Damn…man." With a mean look on Mr. Jed's face, he says, "Shit."

He makes a line mark, indicating five points on a piece of dirty, old, plain paper with a pencil. He studies his dominos in his hand. "Oh yeah!" He slams his domino down; that gives him ten points. "Take that!" he yells out.

Trump Junior is speaking on the snowy TV screen.

"Hey, Jed," says Dexter.

"What's on your mind, old fuck?"

"Don't call me an old fuck, you old fuck!" Mr. Dexter yells out. "I went on a little R & R when I went back into the world. Man… America ain't what it used to be," says Dexter.

"What'd you mean, Dexter?"

"Jed, I'm glad, I'm a ghost here in Oak Wood. The world has gone crazy, downright mad."

"In what way, Dexter?" asks Mr. Jed.

"Do you know, Jed, that there's this guy who's supposedly running the White House and looks just like the fool on the telly there, startin' all kinds of chaos in the country? And that (*pointing to the TV*) crook has been lying to the living American people from day 1. He pardons all his political cronies. They say he's a racist! He's a coward because he's afraid to stand up against that guy in Russia."

"You talkin' about *Pootang*?"

"You mean Putin, don't cha?"

"No. I meant what I said."

They both laugh.

"And I heard that a young teenager *killed* two people at a protest, walked in the middle of the darn street with his weapon hanging on his shoulder, passing right by the police, and they didn't do a freakin' thing to the little piece of shit. Instead, the kid gets praises from that guy in the White House."

"No…shit," says Jed.

"Oh…you ain't heard the worst of it."

"What else is there, Dexter?"

"This fool was caught saying that he could grab women by their you know what, and they liked it."

"*No!*" says Jed.

"A young lady can't even be in her own home without getting killed by police who claims that something was going on in her home or somethin' like that, man. Because of that guy in the White House, America is in turmoil and chaos. Don't know what to make of it, Jed."

"I am so disappointed in the way that guy has brought our country down to a new low," says Jed.

"Well…maybe he wants to make America great," says Dexter. "Shit…if that's what he thinks he's doing…somebody needs to bring his butt to pay a visit to Oak Wood Cemetery and let us give him a rude awakening and show him how he's screwing up America," says Dexter.

"Damn, shame. Damn, shame," says Jed.

"People ain't like the way we used to be when we were among the living, Jed. Nope," says Dexter. "I was on ghost Internet channel the other day, and guess what I saw, Jed?"

"What did you see, my friend?"

"There was this gorgeous-looking African American woman who was dressed in her American colors, red, white, and blue jumpsuit in a cab, going somewhere. The cabdriver asked her who she was supporting. The woman said she was supporting Trump. The cabdriver tried to enlighten the young woman on how Trump and his cronies hated people of color and all the bad things that have occurred in his administration in this country toward people of color.

"The woman was not having it and didn't care what has happened in the pass or anything about Trump. The cabdriver pulled his cab over to the curb and said '*get out* of my cab.'

"The young woman was shocked. 'Why?' she asked the cabdriver.

"'Because anyone who doesn't care about their race and supports a man who cares less about their race and supports such a person like Trump…does not deserve to ride in my cab. *Get out…now.*'

"'But! But! I-I—' she tried to say.

"'I your butt outta my cab,' said the cabdriver.

"She got out, slamming the car door. The cab sped off.

"Good cabdriver," says Dexter.

"Yep," replies Jed.

They both laugh.

"So glad I'm a ghost so I don't have to be afraid of what's going on back in the world, man. I can breathe," says Dexter.

"Me too," replies Jed. "What'd you mean you can breathe? You're dead, and the dead don't need to breathe."

"C'mon…man, play and try not to think about it, Jed."

"Yeah…maybe you're right, but I just can't help it, Dexter. I'm gonna keep my ass right here in the graveyard. I don't need no R & R back in a world with all that drama and hate," says Jed.

Dexter slams a domino on the tree stump. "Give me five!" Dexter yells out.

"Fuck," replies Jed.

"You know, Jed?"

"Know what, Dexter?"

"I'm so glad ain't no racism here in Oak Wood Cemetery," says Dexter.

"What are you talking about, buddy?"

"I mean…ain't no racism here among us ghost."

"Really? What made you come to that marvelous conclusion?" asks Jed.

"Well, as long as I've been here, waiting to make my final transition, which has been a long fucking death time…I ain't ever seen a trace of ghosts showing racism or any other animosity to one another."

"And why do you think it's so, Dex?"

"Look, we have to die, get buried here in this cemetery, and our souls are here, resting in peace. No drama…no fightin'…just peace, quiet, and sex."

"*Sex!*" Jed yells out.

"Yep."

"You can't have no sex. You're a ghost," replies Jed.

"When there's a will…there's a way," says Dexter.

"Hmm," replies Jed, "you still don't get it, do you, Dexter?"

"I'm tryin'."

"Okay, look at me and tell me what you see," says Jed.

Dexter looks at Jed. "I see you," says Dexter.

"I know that…but what color of me do you see?"

"Hell, you ain't got no color. You're a ghost and a transparent ghost at that," says Dexter.

"Exactly…you don't see my human color. You just see right through me, and I see right through you. I can't see your human White skin…being dead and all. We ghosts are transparent and don't have color, therefore no racism, no hatin'…no nothin', just gettin' along with each other like two peas in a pod," says Jed.

Staring down at the dominos, Dexter says, "Well, I guess you have a point, buddy. Damn skippy."

"*Slam!*" Mr. Jed yells out as his domino gives himself another ten points as Dexter studies his next move.

"Hey, Dex?"

"Yeah, Jed?"

"I love you, man," says Jed.

"Bashfully, you knucklehead," says Dexter. "You know, Jed, I like this new series coming on your TV *This Is Your Life*."

On the TV screen, an episode of *This Is Your Life* is being shown.

"They're shooting a new type of that series down there at Grave Stone Productions called *This Was Your Life*," says Mr. Dexter.

"No shit," replies Mr. Jed.

Creadel and Lil Candy are passing by them, overhearing the conversation.

"How you all doing, Mr. Dexter and Mr. Jed?" yells Lil Candy.

"Evenin'," says Mr. Dexter.

Jed just nods.

"Jed's cheating," says Mr. Dexter.

"I ain't cheatin'!" Mr. Jed yells out.

"You are too! I oughta smack yah," says Mr. Dexter.

"You know, ain't no violence here in this graveyard, Dex."

They both laugh.

"You couldn't do no such thing, baldie, 'cause you're a freakin' ghost, and ghosts can't feel on another, got no feelings."

Mr. Dexter laughs. "Shit…don't temp me."

"You know, Mable over on Grave Avenue made her final transition the other day," says Jed.

"No…shit. She's gone?"

"Yep, man, she went in style," says Jed.

"How did she leave?" asks Dexter.

"She had a horse-drawn carriage she sat in, and it went off into the dark night of gray clouds and stars," says Jed.

"Well…I'll be…," responds Dexter.

Still walking down the paved road, Creadel and Lil Candy hear music filtering in closer to them. Three young transparent girl ghosts are jumping rope as Creadel and Lil Candy are passing by them. One is a transparent Caucasian little girl who has dead-gray skin with a deep cut on the side of her face. She is wearing rotten plaid dress, dirty white socks, pigtails, and black shoes as she turns the rope. At the other end of the rope is a transparent Japanese ghost girl. Her skin is decomposed to her skeletal body frame. She's wearing decayed Japanese attire. Half of her head and face are missing, and she's turning the rope. The third little ghost girl jumping rope is African American, wearing rotten blue jeans, red T-shirt, and barefooted. Her left arm has been severed off. She is missing an eye out of her right eye socket.

Five hundred feet from them is the Mazo La Voodoo Mausoleum Store. Inside this particular mausoleum are all sorts of voodoo paraphernalia, various types of magic potions, rabbit's foot with small chains hanging on the racks inside, and also chicken feet. Various types of voodoo dolls for all occasions and jars of animals then line the walls inside. Alligator heads of various sizes are scattered around the mausoleum.

There's a karma keeper voodoo doll with seven custom ritual skulls with voodoo pins stuck on it. Dead snakes are enclosed in jars with liquid substance in them. There are also many special New Orleans voodoo dolls representing green for good luck, power, money, wealth, prosperity, and revenge. It also sells seven-inch day candles used to protect from enemies or to bring wealth. There's a voodoo priestess in her forties, with dreadlock hair and African attire, and the ghosts call her VooDoo Black Mamba who looks like an old woman zombie with cold-gray eyes.

Off in the distance, ahead of them, there's a mausoleum with a neon sign above the entrance that reads Club of Souls. Music can be heard from within.

"You hear that?" asks Lil Candy.

"What?" asks Creadel.

"The music coming from the mausoleum Club of Souls over there," says Lil Candy. The music she hears is by Fred Westley & The JB's "Doing It to Death" 1973 version.

"I hear it," says Creadel.

"C'mon, we're gonna have a fuckin' good time at Club of Souls," says Lil Candy as she drags Creadel by his arm toward the Club of Souls.

The two of them cut across the graveyard to the mausoleum club. Ghosts are entering.

"Hold up," says Creadel. "This mausoleum is just a small room that has a coffin inside," says Creadel.

"Maybe, but wait until you see the inside," says Lil Candy.

"It's not big enough to hold a lot of souls or ghosts," says Creadel.

"It may be small in appearance on the outside, but when you enter the inside, it's much larger than you think, like in real life," says Lil Candy. "Just wait until we go inside the place and you will see for yourself." She's dragging him inside the club.

Inside the Club of Souls, the theme is that of the 1960s. Half round leather booths with small lamps in the center of the round table are lined along the walls. Tables are covered with burgundy linen to match the chairs. Drinking glasses with liquor in them sit in front of the ghosts. There are bottles of liquor and ashtrays with lit cigarettes in them, making the room smoky. Ghosts dressed up in evening attire sit in the booths and at tables around the room. Ghosts and skeletons are dancing on the dance floor in front of a stage. A big band is playing "Doing It to Death" by James Brown. The singer—a transparent African American male ghost in his forties with processed hair that's laid back, wearing a white suit and bow tie and white shoes—is standing at an old-style square microphone, singing. Female ghost divas are cheering him along the front of the stage; one even faints. The saxophonist is blowing his part of "Doing It to Death."

The dance floor is full of ghosts, steppin'. A voluptuous female ghost—Caucasian, in her fifties, wearing a tight-fitting dress, has short blond hair, busty, and wearing a red lipstick and rouge on her cheeks—is dancing with a male African American transparent ghost in his fifties. His head is bald with stitches from his ear across his forehead. He is dressed in a black pinstriped suit with bloodstained white shirt and tie. His face and body are decomposed. The two of them has the crowd amazed as they do their steppin' dance for them to see. The music changes to Funkadelic's "Knee Deep."

Creadel and Lil Candy are walking off the dance floor.

"Wow…that is amazing," says Creadel.

"I know," replies Lil Candy. "Let's find us a table," she says.

They walk through the crowd of dancing ghosts to a booth and sit. In the center of the table is a small lamp-style light to illuminate the table area only. They slide into the booth. They stare out into the dancing ghosts on the dance floor.

"Man, this is nice," says Creadel.

"Yes, it is," replies Lil Candy.

A female transparent waitress ghost named Sylvia is carrying a tray with transparent drinks. The waitress approaches their table. She is dressed in a rotten green miniskirt and green blouse showing her cleavage. Her hair is in dreadlocks. She's wearing red lipstick. Her skin is dead-gray, and there's a blood stain at the center of her blouse. She has a cigarette stuck in the side of her mouth as she sits her tray on Creadel's table.

"Hey, folks. I'm Sylvia, and I'm your waitress for the night. What can I get, you fine spirits?"

"Can I get an I Put a Spell on You with a dead lemon twist?" asks Lil Candy.

"What would you like, sir?"

"You got any weed?" asks Creadel.

"Weed? I'll see what I can dig up," says Sylvia. "I'll be right back," she says as she walks away.

"C'mon, Creadel, let's dance."

Lil Candy pulls Creadel onto the dance floor by his hand, and they start dancing.

As the night goes on, the two of them are enjoying each other and having fun in the Club of Souls. It's five o'clock in the morning, and ghosts are leaving the club as it shuts down. Creadel and Lil Candy are standing at her grave.

"I had a great time tonight, Creadel."

"Yeah, me too," Creadel replies.

Lil Candy looks down at her grave with a few dead flowers by her headstone. "You wanna come down?" she asks. Creadel laughs. "I'll show you the new…and improved…Candy."

"Are you askin' me to have sex with you, woman, after all these years and both of us are dead as hell?" asks Creadel.

"Well…after all…you introduced me to playing house that way…back then…and now I'm addicted to, you know what, sucking," says Lil Candy.

"Don't say it, Lil Candy. I get your point."

"Back then, you…it…hadn't grown up…yet. But I was able to manage with it," says Lil Candy.

"I guess you did. I don't remember you complaining back then," says Creadel.

"So you don't want to play? Have an experience from the past?"

"Not tonight, Lil Candy, not tonight."

"Well, you don't know what you're missing. You sure you don't want to change your mind?"

"I'm sure."

"Okay, then! Don't forget about going with me to Grave Stone Studio later on," says Lil Candy.

"Just come to my plot and get me," says Creadel.

"Okay. I will."

Lil Candy's ghost steps on her grave and dissolves into it. Creadel walks to his grave and does the same thing.

# CHAPTER 5

It's nine o'clock in the evening in Oak Wood Cemetery. The graveyard is alive and well with ghosts going about their regular activities in the cemetery. A male ghost—in his forties, Chinese, with long black ponytail, dressed in a stripped orange-and-white prison uniform, with handcuffs hanging on his left wrist and shackles on his ankles—pokes his face out of a mausoleum jailhouse with steel-barred doorway and prison bars on the window. He cautiously steps out of the mausoleum. He tiptoes behind the mausoleum out of sight, making his nighttime escape.

Lil Candy is approaching Creadel's grave. She stares down at it. She kicks Creadel's headstone. The headstone glows.

"Who is it?" Creadel yells from beneath the dirt covering his grave.

"It's me, Lil Candy! Time to rise and shine. Time to go, Creadel! Come on up! We gotta go to Grave Stone Productions early so we can get some good seats!" yells Lil Candy.

"Okay! Be right up!"

Moments later, Creadel's soul slowly rises from beneath the dirt covering his grave and stands in front of Lil Candy. "Okay, here I am. You ready?" asks Creadel.

"Yeah, come on."

They walk down the asphalt paved road to Grave Stone Productions Co., a mausoleum where there is a long line of ghosts waiting to get inside, ghosts from various time periods.

"Man, we gotta stand in this long-ass line?" asks Creadel.

"No, we don't," says Lil Candy. "I've got the hookup, just follow my lead."

Lil Candy, dressed in her red leather miniskirt and matching jacket vest, goes to the front of the line where a security ghost is standing with a clipboard and a roll of numbered tickets to give to the ghosts that he let inside the production mausoleum.

The security—a male ghost, a little chubby, in his forties, Caucasian, with the front of his nose missing, and dressed in his security uniform and cap—is watching Lil Candy and Creadel approach him.

"How you doing, Mr. Security?" asks Lil Candy.

"I'm doing just fine, Lil Candy. How about you?"

"Oh…I guess…I'm good. You think I'm good…handsome?" Lil Candy pushes her boobs up a little to entice him.

"Hell yeah," says the security ghost.

"You got me on the list, you handsome devil?"

The security guard blushes. He chuckles a little. "Let me check the list, fine as wine just my kind," says the security. He fingers down the clipboard list. "Naw…don't see you on here," he says.

"Shit," says Creadel.

Lil Candy steps close to the security guard's ear and whispers, "If you let me and my friend in…I'll think about us going to your grave plot next week."

A big smile comes on his face. "Well, I'll be damned. I do see your name at the bottom of this here, Lil Candy." He hands both Lil Candy and Creadel a numbered ticket and opens the door to let them inside. There are lots of grumbling in the long line of ghosts watching them entering.

"So why are we here in this studio?" asks Creadel.

"They need some background ghosts for a new episode of *This Was Your Life*," says Lil Candy.

"Oh, you mean background actors, don't cha?" asks Creadel.

"That's what they're calling it these days when you're dead, Creadel." says Lil Candy.

"Oh," replies Creadel.

Inside the mausoleum is a real full-scale production studio, complete with all the production equipment, cameras, and busy ghost crew, preparing the set for the show's next episode of *This Was*

*Your Life*. On one side of the set is a large round vertical spinning wheel with numbers on it. To the side of the large spinning wheel is a square gold-plated large tray with large black cards with the words "This Was Your Life" printed on the front.

Across from the set are long rows of bleachers for ghosts and skeletons to sit. A large neon sign with flashing lights and the words "This Was Your Life" is mounted and flashing above on the wall behind the bleachers with long curtains and also on the wall behind the set.

Creadel and Lil Candy walk to the rows of bleachers. They sit and stare at the production set in amazement.

"Wow…this is really something," says Creadel.

"Sure is," replies Lil Candy.

Ghosts and skeletons are starting to enter and fill the bleachers around them.

"Let's get our seats on the front row here," says Lil Candy.

"Okay."

The two of them sit in the center of the first row in front of the production set. Lots of ghosts and skeletons from various time periods are seating among them. The director is sitting in her producer's chair behind two monitors showing the set, giving directions to the crew.

Creadel and Lil Candy are sitting, watching the crew work.

"So what happened to you, Lil Candy, that got you here?" asks Creadel.

"My heart," she says.

"Your heart?"

"Yes."

"I died of a broken heart," says Lil Candy.

"Wow…sorry to hear that," says Creadel. "What happened?"

"Well…one night, I went home and found my boo fucking my mother. My mother…fucking my boo. Both of them fuckers fuckin' over me! My heart couldn't take the strain, and I kicked the bucket.

"The next thing I knew, a ghost was waking my butt up in this crazy-ass graveyard society here in Oak Wood Cemetery. How about you?" asks Lil Candy.

"Hell, I guess I must have had a massive dose of cancer and blacked out. The next thing I knew, some woman spirit brought me here, and I was watching them put my coffin into the ground."

"Oh…wow," replies Lil Candy.

"Quiet on the set!" the director yells out.

"*Lights!*" The set lights are lowered.

"*Cameras!*" Cameras start rolling.

"And *action*!"

The hostess, Nikki, is an attractive African American female ghost with a shapely body dressed in a tight-fitting dress with a slit down the right side. Her skin is dark, dead-gray complexion. Her waist is small, and her chest is very busty. Her eyelashes are long, eyebrows arch perfectly, and her makeup is flawless. Her hair is platinum with an orchid stuck in the left side of her hair as she walks onto the set. A neon sign above the set flashes off and on for the ghosts to applaud. The ghosts start applauding.

*On the Set*

"Welcome to another episode of…*This…Was…Your…Life!*

"I'm your hostess, Nikki!"

"Hubba-hubba," says Creadel.

"Really…Creadel," says Lil Candy. "I mean, you're hubbanizin' over Nikki over there, and here I am (*she stands up in front of Creadel, runs her hands down the side of her body, and bends a little so he gets a good look at her butt*) right here beside you, willin', able, and…more than damn…ready to play. You ain't up for this (*rubbing her butt*)?"

Just as Creadel is about to respond, the ghost audience applauds.

"Okay! You all know how this show works," says Nikki. "You all have been given a ticket upon entering with a number on it. I will spin the numbers wheel three times, and all you have to do is match your number with the number the spinning wheel stops on. Sounds…like fun…I know," says hostess Nikki.

"Now…let's get the show started." Nikki walks closer to the large spinning wheel and spins it around. The wheel spins and closely comes to a stop on the number 0. "The first number is zero." The audience of ghosts checks their ticket number as does Lil Candy. Creadel, looking disinterested, drops his ticket on the floor by his foot. Nikki spins the wheel again. Again, the wheel comes to a close stop on zero. "We have another zero!" Nikki yells out.

"Shit!" says Lil Candy. She notices Creadel not looking at his ticket. "Creadel, why're you not checking your ticket?" Lil Candy asks.

"Hell, I ain't got no winning ticket, Lil Candy. That's the way my luck runs," says Creadel.

"You don't know that," says Lil Candy.

"And…for the last spin." Nikki gives the wheel one last big spin. Everyone's eyes are glued to the wheel as it makes its last stop on the number 7. "And the last lucky number is seven!" Nikki yells out.

"Damn, not me," says Lil Candy, looking at her ticket. "Where's your ticket, Creadel?"

Lil Candy spots his ticket on the floor by his feet and picks it up. She stares at his numbers on the ticket. She is in shock. Hysterically, she says, "We got it! We got it!" She is jumping up and down, screaming. "Your ticket, Creadel! You got the winning ticket, boo!" Creadel is in shock and very surprised. Lil Candy sticks the ticket in Creadel's hand. The audience of ghosts applauds them.

"C'mon…down…winning ticket 7!" Nikki Barber yells out.

"I'm shy," says Creadel. Lil Candy pushes him up onto the floor. Creadel walks to Nikki and hands her his lucky winning ticket. Lil Candy is cheering him on!

"Have a seat on the sofa here, ticket 7," says Nikki.

Creadel sits and stares at the audience of ghosts and at Lil Candy in the bleachers. He's a celebrity now. Nikki shakes his hand.

"What's your name, sir?"

"Creadel, Creadel Jones."

"Well, Creadel Jones, welcome to *This Was Your Life*!"

The neon sign above flashes. Ghosts audience applauds.

"Now the way this show works is that I will enter your name in our *This Was Your Life* computer, and the computer will print out your life's history in which I will choose three outstanding acts you did when you were alive back in the world, you understand, Mr. Jones?"

"Yes."

A computer with a printer rolls out a long, long, long sheet of Creadel's life's history to a female skeleton making it work. The skeleton woman is dressed in high heels and floral dress. On her skeleton head is her red wig; her eyeballs are still in its sockets with wire-framed eyeglasses. She detaches the long sheets of paper and hands them to Nikki and does her sexy stroll back off the set. Nikki looks up and down the long sheets.

"Hmm," Nikki says.

Creadel and Lil Candy look curiously at Nikki.

Hostess Nikki is looking over a long, long spreadsheet and running her right finger down and up the sheets of paper. "Hmm…you did this…you did that…you did…this. You did…that. Hmm…I see…you had lots…of sex. Boy, you did a lot of freakin'—okay. It seems…that you have been a very busy person. You like a lotta sex… more sex…more sex…good God…man, you like doin' the nasty a lot," says Nikki. "You've lived a good life by all accounts. You were a good human being when you were living in the real world. You lived a straight and righteous life. You did some very great things. Okay."

A sign of relief comes on to Creadel's face.

"I have chosen three outstanding events, even though you have done many, that you should be rewarded for, sir. Drop the screen, please!" host Nikki yells out.

An eight-feet screen is lowered from the ceiling in front of the audience. The words "This Was Your Life" appears on the white screen in glittery large letters. She toys around with the computer. Nikki walks to Creadel who is watching the large screen being lowered.

The first *This Was Your Life* event is this one. Do you recall this event, Mr. Jones? Roll it!" Nikki yells.

A video comes onto the screen.

"You were in California on your way to work. You were walking downtown on Seventh Street and Broadway where you saw a homeless woman trying to keep her naked behind from being seen by people walking past her with newspaper. You remember that night, Mr. Creadel?"

"Yes, I do."

"Now…tell our audience what went through your mind at that time, sir."

"Well…I wondered what happened to her that got her in the situation she was in. I felt sorry for her, and I said to myself that the next paycheck I get, I will take one hundred dollars and give it to her the next time I see her."

The video on the screen shows Creadel doing just that the next time he saw the homeless woman, giving her a hundred-dollar bill.

Lil Candy is looking teary-eyed.

"That was so nice and thoughtful of you, Mr. Jones. You have a good heart," says Nikki. "On a different night going to work in downtown Los Angeles, you were on a city transit bus. A homeless man entered, wearing nothing but a pair of dirty pants on that cold winter night. What did you do, sir?"

"I took off my coat and gave it to him," says Creadel.

"Not only do you have a heart but you also have compassion," says Nikki.

The audience applauds again.

Words appear on the screen: third event.

"On this particular day, on the southside of Chicago, the video starts showing on-screen a little toddler walking unattended down a neighborhood sidewalk," says Nikki.

"Yeah…I remember that day. I was in my car driving when I saw this toddler with no one near her walking and about to turn the corner toward an alley about eighty feet away. I pulled my car over to the curve quickly because I was afraid the baby was going to be hit by a car coming out the alley. I got out my car and looked for someone to see me and help me get this baby to safety. One lady was talking to somebody in a parked car down the middle of the block and looked at me like I was crazy. She didn't see the toddler walking. I saw the baby getting closer to the alley, so I kept calling her to come back to me.

"By this time, a lady from a house across the street from where I was, who saw what was going on, came over to me. The baby did come to me. I looked down the street, and out of a front door of someone's house, five house down, came some guy on his cell phone to get the baby. The baby had opened the fence gate and started walking down the sidewalk by herself. The lady from across the street and I just shook our heads in disbelief."

"You saved that toddlers life, Mr. Jones, because if you hadn't been there at the right time, that baby might not be living this day. You saved a life, Mr. Jones," says Nikki.

Audience applauds.

"Okay…and now the fourth event," says Nikki.

This next event is very significant. The large projector screen begins to show Creadel driving his car from the loop on Cottage Grove, going southbound, heading home. The video freezes.

"You remember this day, Sir Creadel?" asks Nikki.

Creadel ponders a few seconds. "Oh…yes. That particular morning, on my way home, I was listening to the radio. Chicago's radio station V-103 let a crying grandmother call out for help on the air for her grandson. In her crying voice, she was begging for anyone with O positive blood to please come to the hospital and give that type of blood to her grandson who might die without it because the hospital didn't have that type of blood," Creadel tells.

"And what happened next, Mr. Jones?" asks Nikki.

"Well, I immediately headed to the hospital where her son needed my type of blood and donated it to help his illness. I went several times after that."

"Wow…what a caring person you are," says Nikki.

"It was nothing. Glad to have did it," says Creadel.

"And what happened after that?" asks Nikki.

"I kept donating my blood to him for weeks, months. Bought him a toy firetruck. I couldn't see him or give it to him personally, so I gave it to his mother, and she was very thankful."

The ghost audience applauds.

"I don't know what happened to him after that, just hoped that he is still living and well."

"And you never heard anything about his condition or health after that?"

"No."

Hostess Nikki paces back and forth a few times, rubbing her chin, thinking. "Hmmm…Mr. Creadel Jones, whether you realize it or not, you, Creadel Jones, saved lives and cared for people in need. For your good endeavors of doing good thing for humanity…for that, Creadel Jones, you no longer have to return into the dirty…deep…soil of your cold and dark grave. Our show *This Was Your Life*…will build you your own customed-designed mausoleum…complete with free Wi-Fi, free cable service, and a fifty-five-inch TV, and…you'll get a brand-new…candy-apple-red coffin," says hostess Nikki.

"Wow," says Creadel.

"Is there anything you would like to have…or do…Mr. Jones?"

Creadel thinks long and hard. The clock is ticking, *ticktock*, ticking loudly…*ticktock, ticktock, ticktock.*

Creadel looks at Lil Candy. "Can I ask a question?" says Creadel.

"Yes. Ask away," says Nikki.

"If I wanted to go back into the world to see some people, do some crazy things, or even be different than what I am…with maybe…a few special gifts or powers…can that happen?" asks Creadel.

"Why…of course," says Nikki. "It will be your world."

"And can I take another ghost with me of my choosing?"

"I don't see why not."

"Okay, okay, okay. There are a few people back in the world I'd like to pay a visit too," says Creadel.

"Is that what you want, Mr. Jones?"

"Yes," replies Creadel.

"Well…let's see if our ghost audience approves of your request by applauding," says hostess Nikki. "Audience! If you approve of his request, applaud and stand up!"

The ghost audience all stand up, applauding, including Lil Candy with a big smile on her face.

"Congratulations! Because you lived a good life and did good things for others, you are hereby granted a *This Was Your Life/Back into the Life* pass."

Henry Mancini's theme of the *Pink Panther* fill the room. The same skeletal female woman who brought out the computer comes back on the set, dancing to the music, carrying a large envelope with Creadel's pass inside. Hostess Nikki takes the envelope with the words "This Was Your Life / Back into the Life Pass" printed on the front. Nikki hands it to Creadel who is very happy. He takes it and walks back to Lil Candy. She plants a big, long kiss on his lips. They walk out of Grave Stone Production Studio arm in arm.

Walking back through the graveyard, Creadel asks, "You want to roll with me, Lil Candy?"

"I thought you'd never ask…Of course, I'll roll with you, boo. Can we play house when we get back in the world?"

"Will…you give it a rest, Lil?"

"Hell, I've been giving it a rest so long it's gotten cobwebs on it," says Lil Candy.

"Really," says Creadel. "Here's your plot. I'll see you in a few hours so we can take our journey back into the world," says Creadel.

"Okay, see you later."

Standing at her grave, she lies on top of it, and her soul dissolves into the grass on her grave. Creadel walks to his grave and does the same thing.

# CHAPTER 6

The early darkness of the morning in Oak Wood Cemetery is very windy. Dust, tumbleweeds, and debris blow in between the graves. Off in the distance, four transparent ghosts, one Caucasian female and three Caucasian men, dressed in 1940's attire, rise from beneath the ground, and the theme from *The Good, the Bad and the Ugly* starts.

A Western gunslinger stands on one end of the graveyard road, staring at his enemy, a gun-toting 1800's gunslinger. The forty-year-old gun-toting gangster ghost has a wide-brimmed, black cowboy hat on over his long blond hair; his hat is dirty with a bullet hole in the center of it and a trickle of dried blood on it. His shaky hand rests on his gold-plated 38 revolver stuck inside his shoulder holster.

The gunslinger is an old-timer with a thick mustache that curves upward at the tips. He's Caucasian, bowlegged, and wearing his cowboy boots with spurs, cowboy shirt and vest, and jeans with holes in the knees. His leather vest has a few bullet holes already. His eyebrows are frizzy. He's chewing tobacco as his long blond hair is blown in the wind. His bloodstained shirt is ripped on the right side. His eyes never blink as he stares at his archenemy at the opposite end of the road. He spits his tobacco out and wipes his mouth with the sleeve of his shirt.

Meanwhile, at the opposite end of the road is a modern-day transparent gangster with an Italian accent resembling actor Al Pacino in *The Godfather*. The gangster is in his forties, dressed in a rotten black suit and black tie with holes all over the suit. The wind is blowing, making his suit coat sway to the side, showing his gold-plated 38 stuck in its shoulder holster. He has a long bloody scar on the left side of his face as he stares back at the gunslinger. The wind sways his wide-brimmed gangster hat. With a cigarette stuck on the side of his mouth, he blows out a puff of smoke. He snatches the cigarette out and flicks it over to the right of him on the grass. Off to the gangster's left side, off the graveyard, the orchestra plays the theme of *The Godfather*.

With the wind blowing, the gunslinger takes one step toward the gangster. The gangster takes one step toward the gunslinger. The gunslinger takes another step. The gangster takes another step toward him. All the cemetery residential ghosts line both sides of the graveyard road to witness the shoot-out. With the theme from *The Godfather* still being heard, they approach each other, *step* by *step* until they're at a distance of fifty feet from each other.

The gunslinger spits out his tobacco again, this time hitting a ghost dog in the eye. The dog growls and runs off. Along the road, standing with the ghosts, are two old female granny ghosts making bets on who's the quickest. Granny Goodrich—eighty, with no teeth, has long gray hair, has boobs sagging on her stomach, has holes in her stockings with one sliding down on her right leg—nudges her transparent ghost friend La Dana Dana Dana, who has red lips, long eyelashes, and rotten plaid dress and is missing her left eye.

"I got five on the bowlegged fella!" says Granny Goodrich.

"You got five on what? Teethless?" asks La Dana Dana Dana.

"I got five on the bowlegged gunslinger fella," says Granny Goodrich.

"I'll take *The Godfather* good-lookin' fella down there. He's so darn sexy-lookin'," says La Dana Dana Dana.

"Cool, fool…you're on…bitch!" says Granny Goodrich.

"Who the hell you callin' bitch, hoe!" La Dana Dana Dana yells out.

"You want a beating right here in the middle of the graveyard? Shout out," says La Dana Dana Dana.

"Girlfriend…you know I was just foolin' around withcha, boo," says Granny Goodrich, laughing.

La Dana Dana Dana just stares at her.

"It's high time you and I settle the score, hombre," says gunslinger.

"Yep, I reckon so," says the gangster.

"You shouldn't have talked about the Old West like you did in the barbershop," says the gunslinger.

With an Italian Tonny Montana accent, the gangster says, "Don't you recognize who you're talkin' to...gunslinger?"

"Why hell...can't say that I do...I don't recognize...who...the hell are you supposed to be anyhow?"

"If you don't know...you better ask somebody," says the gangster. "Damn, you're one ugly son of a biscuit eater," says the gangster.

A male ghost kid standing on the side of the road across from them yells out, "He's a member of the Corleone Club!"

"Yah don't...say," says the gunslinger. "That still don't give you the right...to put the West down...hombre. Now...I gotta do the righteous thing," says the gunslinger.

"An what's that, potnah?" asks the gangster.

"I gotta...kill...yah. Now draw."

The gangster starts laughing. "Look here, slinger, we can come to some sort of mutual agreement or somethin'. Ain't got to be no killin', no bloodshed and shootin' and shit," says the gangster.

"I ain't agreein' to nothin'. Gotta respect the laws of the West where I roamed. Gotta do what I gotta do."

"All right, you done pissing me off. Let's do this," says the gangster.

The orchestra starts playing the theme of *The Good, the Bad and the Ugly*.

They both take a few steps backward and stand, ready to draw.

A decayed, transparent male ghost from the eighteenth century standing on the sideline says, "On my count of three, you boys draw." The music intensifies. "*One! Two! Three!*"

Both of the them draw at the same time.

Guns are blazing! Bullets are hitting both their bodies, going right through them. The both of them are staggering and stumbling. The gangster falls to the ground. The gunslinger is still staggering and swaying back and forth. He spits tobacco out again. He stands unsteadily.

Then, suddenly, out of the crowded line of ghosts witnessing the shoot-out, a young twelve-year-old female ghost—resembling Shirley Temple, wearing a rotten white dress with black dots, and has one leg that has a prosthesis—walks onto the center of the road. "Hold…up! Hold! Are y'all gonna kill each other while you're already dead?" the young twelve-year-old female ghost asks.

The gunslinger thinks a minute. "Well…I'll be…you got a point there, young lady."

The gangster ghost stands up. "She does have a point there, gunslinger, I reckon," he says.

"Guess this means we gotta be friends after all," he says.

"I reckon so…I can handle that," says the gangster.

They shake hands and walk away together.

"That was fun, wasn't it, gangster?"

"Yeah, brought back memories of the Old West days."

The orchestra plays the theme of *The Good, the Bad and the Ugly*.

# CHAPTER 7

A few hours later, Oak Wood Cemetery is quiet with only the sound of crickets. The full moon illuminates the many headstones in the graveyard. An owl sits on a tree limb. It scans the ground for prey. Only a few ghosts are still mingling about the graveyard. Creadel and Lil Candy are leaning against a large headstone.

"So what are you going to do, Creadel, with your free pass?"

Creadel ponders a few seconds. "I don't know," he says.

"Well, you have a chance to return to where you came from for a brief period of time," says Lil Candy.

"Yeah, I know. I've been thinking about some things."

"Really? What?"

"Well, for one thing, something has been bothering me for many years."

"Tell me," says Lil Candy.

"Well, have you ever known people who would go to a funeral to pay respect to the dead but instead…they attend the funeral home, stand over the deceased coffin, and, instead of saying farewell, things like…'Rest in peace,' 'You will be missed,' 'Take care, motherfucka,' or something respectful, they would stand over the deceased in the coffin and make derogatory statements in their mind, thinking that the dead can't hear them?" says Creadel.

"I know of some people who said they did that when I was alive back in the world," says Lil Candy. "I suppose people are still doing it," she says.

"Yeah. They are still doing it," says Creadel.

"How do you know, Creadel?"

"Because it happened to me at my funeral."

"Really?" says Lil Candy.

"There I lay, dead as a fucking doornail in my coffin at the funeral home, right? My coffin is open. My body is stiff as cardboard. I couldn't move if a naked woman stood in front of me and hit me in the face with her big, fat-ass titties." Lil Candy laughs. "Most of the people who came to pay respect to me, I didn't even know them. Some of the women was finer than sin too. But, this woman, Glodious, my half sister, came into the funeral home, walked down the aisle, and stood at my coffin. She stared down at my corpse. I know I was lookin' good as all hell in my casket, but for some reason, I could tell her ass was up to no good."

"What's so bad about that? Lots of people come and just stare at the deceased and walk away," says Lil Candy.

"I know…but it was what she was saying to me in her fucked-up mind that was so troublesome. Even though I was dead-ass, she didn't know that my dead soul can hear every word she said and see all."

"What did she say, Creadel?"

Creadel starts looking depressed. "She said some things that were totally wrong, totally untrue, and the woman is very mistaken about what she thought really happened back in the world when we were young siblings. She said some fucked-up shit to me, Lil Candy. She was so…fucking…wrong," says Creadel.

"So are you gonna tell me what she said or what?"

"Forget about it, babe," says Creadel.

"Well, what are you thinking about doing?" asks Lil Candy. "You're going to confront her, aren't you! You're going to go to her and straighten her out about whatever she said wrong to you, right?"

"Well, now that you mentioned it…that would be a good thing to do," says Creadel. "I should set the record straight with her evil ass once and for all.

"All this time…I thought she loved me as a brother, and now she was all fake to me, all an act!" cries Creadel. Creadel starts walking away.

"Okay, where are we going now, baby?"

"We?" asks Creadel.

"Yeah, you and yours truly. You don't think I'm gonna let you deal with her all by yourself, do yah? I'm with you until death do us part…oops or…well, to the end, anyway, babe," says Lil Candy. "And maybe…just maybe…with a little luck…we can play house in the real world for a few hours…before we come back," says Lil Candy.

"Is sex all you think about, Lil Candy?"

"Hell, I'm dead. I can't do nothin' else here as a ghost in Oak Wood Cemetery. It makes you think a lot. Besides, I ain't had none in a long…while. Well, just think about it, will yah!" says Lil Candy.

"I think I know where she is, but we've got to make a stop before we go where she is first."

"Okay, where are we going then?" asks Lil Candy.

"California, gotta see a spook," says Creadel.

"California? A spook! What are you talking about, man?" asks Lil Candy.

"C'mon. I'll tell you on the way. California…here we, ghosts, come."

"How are we going to get there?" she asks.

Creadel just says one word, "Amtrak."

"But we are ghosts," says Lil Candy.

"Exactly, we don't gotta pay because we can't be seen by the conductor's human eye unless we want to be seen," replies Creadel. "And why float when we can ride…free?"

"Aaah," says Lil Candy. "Can we get a sleeper and play house?" she asks.

"Will you give it a rest, please?" says Creadel.

"All right…all right."

They walk down through the cemetery's paved road toward the main entrance's huge green steel gates and leave.

*Few Hours Later*
*Forest Lawn Memorial Park & Mortuary, California*

It's nine o'clock in the cemetery of Forest Lawn Memorial Park. The cemetery is a typical well-manicured graveyard. The headstones outnumber the mausoleums by far. Ghosts are sitting or lying on top of their headstones, and other ghosts are reading transparent newspapers or watching transparent television atop their headstones with a static screen showing the black-and-white TV movie *The Evil Dead*. Some of them are playing cards while ghost kids are playing and running about the graveyard.

Creadel and Lil Candy are entering the front entrance of the cemetery and standing, scanning the yard.

"Okay, will you tell me about the woman standing over your casket, saying evil things to your dead body? You wouldn't tell me what the woman said to you before we left. So at least you can tell me why we had to come all the way out here to a California graveyard. And now that you brought me here…what's up? Who do you know who's laid to rest here?" asks Lil Candy.

"Quinton, my father."

"Oh," says Lil Candy.

"His grave is somewhere around here," says Creadel, pointing out in the graveyard.

The two of them walk through the graveyard, searching the headstones until Creadel stops at a headstone that reads

> In loving memory of
> Vaughn Jones
> 1929–2004

Creadel stares down at his father's grave as Lil Candy stands beside him, checking her makeup in a small mirror. Creadel knocks on the headstone.

No response from his father's grave.

"Come on out, Vaughn! I know you're down there!"

Still no response from the grave.

"Maybe he ain't in there," says Lil Candy.

"I don't know," replies Creadel.

Thirty feet away from them is a male Caucasian ghost, looking very old, looking much like Rip Van Wrinkle with a long white beard, sitting in his transparent rocking chair, staring at a large old hourglass that's slowly dropping one gram of sand to the bottom.

"After all this time, this hourglass only drops when it feels like it. I ain't got much more time to wait on it," the old man says.

The old Rip Van Wrinkle-looking ghost man yells out to them. "He ain't down there! He made his transition long time ago," he tells them.

"Did they take him up or did they take him down?" asks Creadel.

"Ain't sho," says the old male ghost with the long white beard.

"Okay, thanks," says Creadel. "Okay. Let's sit down a spell," says Creadel.

"Tell me what's going on with you, babe?" says Lil Candy.

They sit at his father's grave.

"I needed to ask him, Vaughn, why he didn't like his oldest son, me," says Creadel.

"What? You telling me that your dad didn't like you, Creadel? He loved you, man."

"I thought he did," says Creadel. "But, when I was thirteen, Mom and my pops, Vaughn, had gotten into an argument and was fighting. I tried to stop Vaughn from hitting my mom by getting in between them. He hit me and said that he didn't like me anyway. Hearing him say that to me hurt more than his hit to my face did. I couldn't help but to cry like a little baby."

"Wow," says Lil Candy.

"I never forgot it. It stuck with me all my life, and I never got a chance to ask Vaughn why he hated me so much.

"I loved my dad, and through the years, I never thought about it much. But as I grew older, I realized the things he was doing, playing around with other women in his marriage to my mom. There were days he would not come home, and my mother didn't know where he was. He would lie to her all the time because he would not admit to being with his side woman who had some bastard kids with him. I realized that was why he never wanted me around to see him playing on my mother, but he would be around my stepbrother and stepsister all the time. That was the kind of man he was. He liked my half brother and half sister, Glodious Jones, the woman who stood over my coffin, saying bad things to me."

"Well, maybe it wasn't like you think, Creadel."

"It was," says Creadel. "With both of us being dead now and me being a ghost, I thought I could connect with his soul and give him a chance to explain why he hated me so much. Plus I want him to explain why the hell he took his bastard kids from their mother and brought them to my mother."

"Look, Creadel, that happened in the past. Nothing you can do about it now, even in this presence. It's sad that you had to experience that at such an early age, but you have to try to forget about it, babe."

"Yeah…I know.

"But I also wanted to ask him why he didn't explain things to my half brother and half sister while he was alive. I can never forget that night. It stuck with me all my life."

"Was he married to your mother at the time, Creadel?"

"Yeah. You see, Lil Candy, it was like I told you. I never forgot the cold winter night in St. Louis. Vaughn, one of his male buddies, and I went to some house that snowy, cold night. My dad kicked open the door, and there were several very young kids in this very hot room with no adult attending them while they slept in bed. We went inside the house.

"My father grabbed one little boy, and his friend grabbed one little girl. With the kids in their arms wrapped in blankets, we went back out into the snow and rushed to my mom's house, where he asked my mom to help him take care of his illegitimate kids. I remember that because my mom was so hurt and didn't know what to do. With help and guidance from my mom's family members, she decided to help him raise these kids.

"There I was, staring at two kids whom I had no clue to who they were, and I made the statement that I didn't want them living with us at my young age. Hell, I didn't really mean it at that time. I was a little kid myself. I felt like my whole world was being invaded as any little kid would feel. And the woman who stood at my casket was the little girl, and she never forgot what happened that night and what I said. Glodious grew up hating my mother and giving my mother a hard time every day. My mom was trying to do her best to raise her and her brother while Pops would hardly come home to help her and still played around on her. Glodious even tried to kill her by putting particles of broken glass in my mother's food on her plate, hoping it would kill her.

"Luckily, my mother saw the glittery glass particles of chipped glass in the food on her plate, and Mom didn't eat anything."

"Damn…that's fucked up," says Lil Candy.

"So Glodious, my stepsister, who was standing over my coffin at the funeral home was saying some pretty bad things to me.

"And now I will pay her a visit."

"Wow…Creadel…that's some deep shit, babe."

"I know."

"So that's where we're going next?"

"Yep."

"Okay then, let's roll, baby," says Lil Candy. "How are we going to get to her?" asks Lil Candy. "You know where she's at?"

"Got a pretty good idea where she is," says Creadel.

They stand and wave to the old male ghost in his rocking chair as they leave the cemetery.

"So are we going to travel by plane, train, or automobile?" asks Lil Candy.

"We're going to take the railroad."

"Amtrak."

"No."

"Plane?"

"No, automobile," replies Creadel.

"Why don't we just float there?" asks Lil Candy.

"Because I'm afraid of heights, and I get dizzy," says Creadel.

"Oh, well, Amtrak it is then…to the windy city…it is."

# CHAPTER 8

In the middle of the night, there's a transparent Halloween parade in progress in the cemetery. There's a line of transparent floats with grotesque ghosts dressed in transparent, dirty, rotten, aged attire. There's a different theme for each float. Transparent marching ghost bands are marching between the floats. Transparent skeletons and ghosts clowns on both sides of the paved graveyard road are having fun and giving out small bags of popcorn to the three deep ghosts onlookers and ghost kids along both sides of the parade.

A female ghost name Blondie—who has blond, curly hair, is attractive, in her forties, is Caucasian, is wearing a Playboy Bunny costume—is walking through the graveyard between mausoleums and headstones. She has stitches across her neck with dried blood on it and on the side of her right jaw. She approaches a mausoleum with a young African American transparent female ghost Jessie. Jessie is in her thirties, has one leg, and is missing one eye. Jessie is dressed in rotten jeans and a dingy, holey red blouse. As Blondie passes by her, she notices Jessie reading a book.

"Hi, Jessie."

"Hey, Blondie," says Jessie.

"Whatcha reading, girlfriend?" asks Blondie.

Jessie just holds up the old, dirty, and partially rotten book cover.

Blondie reads the title out loud. "Graveyard Society—if you think you just died…think again." Is it good?" Blondie asks.

"It's a page-turner," replies Jessie.

"Cool."

"You going to the parade, Jessie?"

"Naw…I want to finish this book."

"Okay."

As Blondie walks through the graveyard to the transparent parade, Jessie says, "Nice costume."

Suddenly, the parade comes to an abrupt stop. A loud announcement is heard throughout the graveyard. A male ghost from the eighteenth century, wearing a rotten eighteenth-century attire. The male ghost has decomposed skin and very few strands of hair on top of his bald head. He's running through the graveyard yelling out loud, "Donald Trump has been indicted! He is number 3 to get canned! And…he has been indicted four times! He should get him three *Lincoln lawyers* to try and save him. Trump is toast!"

The ghosts start celebrating in jubilee all over the graveyard. Creadel and Lil Candy have just entered the entrance gates and stare.

"What the hell…is going on here?" asks Creadel.

"I ain't got a clue," replies Lil Candy.

A young male—African American, midget, ghost, in his thirties, with big Afro, in hip-hop attire—is dancing in front of them.

Creadel grabs him by his wrist and asks. "What's going on, sir?" asks Creadel.

"You ain't heard?" the young midget ghost asks.

"No. We just came back. What's happening?" asks Creadel.

"What's the celebration about?" asks Lil Candy.

The midget ghost replies to her. "America has had two presidents to be impeached, and just now there's a third new one… Donald J. Trump (a.k.a. POTUS, the impeached number…three)," says the midget ghost. "And he has four criminal indictments."

"No shit," says Creadel.

"Wow," says Lil Candy.

The midget ghost dances away and disappears among the lines of ghosts celebrating.

"And he thought he was Teflon Don," says Creadel.

"Well, he has a big-ass stain on him for life now when he's call in for his judgment day," says Lil Candy.

Another Caucasian male ghost Jerry Crafton, a present-day ghost dressed in a business suit with bloodstains in the middle of his white shirt and tie, says as he stumps away into the darkness of the graveyard, "Shit! Shit! The damn Democrats just had to do it to Don. Fuck! Unfair! Inaccurate counts! They should do a damn recount!"

Creadel and Lil Candy stare at him walking away in frustration. The parade resumes.

*****

Meanwhile, there's a house party and card game going on at Creadel's stepsister Glodious's house on the west side of Chicago. Glodious's house is an old bungalow. The small house is a double-story with a sloping roof and a porch with four young men, two Caucasian and two African American, who are smoking pot, drinking cans of beer on the steps, and sitting on the front porch concrete ledge. All of them are dressed in jeans and white T-shirts, baseball caps, and tennis shoes. The house has a small front yard.

Glodious comes out the front door of her house. She stands on the front porch, looking over her neighborhood. It was dark; the street was quiet except for the DJ's music being played inside. She walks to one of the young men smoking a joint. She takes it from his mouth and takes a draw on it herself.

"Wow...this is some good...shit, man," says Glodious.

"I know," replies the young man named Jake.

Jeff, Glodiuos's husband, comes to the front door and looks at Glodious. "Babe, Janice wants to know if you have an extra blouse. She spilled something on hers."

"Yeah. I'll be right in," says Glodious. She hands back the joint to Jake and enters the house.

The house is full of her friends dancing, playing Bidwiz, and having drinks. A DJ is playing steppers music. Couples are in front of the DJ's setup, dancing. In one of the rooms, there are long tables of soul food: barbecue ribs, fried chicken wings, potato salad, a large bowl of spaghetti, and a tray of dinner rolls. Paper plates, forks, spoons, and plastic knives are placed in the center of the long table along with napkins.

Glodious is dressed in a white floral print tight dress. She has a long black ponytail. She has on white tennis shoes. She and her husband, Jeff—a dark-complexioned man in his fifties, with short Afro, wearing black pants and white shirt—are among several people in the center of the living room doing the electric slide to the DJ's music.

*****

Back at Oak Wood Cemetery, it's quiet as the sun begins to set in the West. A few hours later, it's dark with only a few light poles illuminating the graveyard. Creadel rises from his grave. He stretches and yawns. His black burial suit is dirty and rotten with holes along with the white shirt he was buried in. He laces up his dirty black shoes as he looks around the cemetery. He notices Lil Candy is not sitting atop her grave. He walks to her grave and hears moaning and groaning deep down in her grave.

"Lil Candy! You down there? What are you doing down there?"

She doesn't answer. He knocks in her headstone a few times.

Still no answer, just moans and groans.

"I hear you down there! You doing something you ain't got no business doin! What are you doing down there, Lil Candy!"

Lil Candy says in frustration, "Jesus…Christ…can't a girl have a little dead me time in her own grave?"

"Me time…does that mean…what I think it means?" Creadel asks.

Lil Candy rises from beneath her grave, looking frustrated. "Just don't worry about what I'm doing. It's my own B-U-S-I-N-E-S-S."

"All right, all right. Calm down," says Creadel.

"I'm calm."

"You ready to go with me to my sista's place?" asks Creadel.

"Yeah," replies Lil Candy.

"Okay."

Lil Candy's wearing a short miniskirt with a slit on the right side of her thigh. Her white blouse is a little dirty. Her fishnet stockings has holes on the left knee and the upper right thigh. Creadel is in front of her as they start walking. She smells the fingers of her right hand as he walks in front of her.

"Where does she live?" asks Lil Candy.

"On the West Side," Creadel replies.

"On the west side of the graveyard?" asks Lil Candy.

"No…the West Side of Chicago," replies Creadel. "We're gonna hitch a ride on the L train to the West Side where she lives," says Creadel.

"Okay," says Lil Candy.

# CHAPTER 9

Glodious's neighborhood is quiet as the sun begins to set. A young teenage newspaper boy is delivering the early morning *Chicago Sun-Times* newspaper from his bicycle. He pulls a copy of the *Chicago Sun-Times* out of his dingy white cloth bag and folds it into a square shape. He aims it for the front porch of Glodious's house. He throws it, and the newspaper lands at the doorway of the house. The sound of the newspaper hitting the bottom of the front screen door wakes up Glodious as she lies next to her husband, Jeff, in bed.

The ground is covered with snow and ice as the newspaper boy tries to ride his bike cautiously on to his next delivery.

The inside of Glodious's bedroom has contemporary furniture, a king-sized bed with dark-brown dresser and large mirror to match. Dark-brown curtains hangs from the top of her bedroom window to the carpeted beige-colored floor. The nightstand has a picture of them, with a lamp and an ashtray with marijuana butts in it. Their clothes and shoes lie next to the bed.

Glodious is lying in bed, wearing nothing but her bra and panties. She just stares up at the ceiling fan that is slowly spinning. Jeff is wearing his boxer brief as Glodious slides her hand inside them. She slowly strokes him. Lying on his back, Jeff's eyes slowly open.

"Damn, baby, that's a good way to wake a man up in the morning," he says.

She turns on her side to face him as she keeps massaging his manhood that is fully erect.

"Don't say anything. I just want you to enjoy this," says Glodious. She throws the white satin sheets cover back to the foot of the bed. She mounts Jeff's erection and starts to ride it until her body is in ecstasy.

After riding it a while, she stands up in the bed, turns around with her back to his face, and squats down on his penis and continues to ride it slowly. Both Glodious and Jeff are moaning at the same time. Jeff's hands are squeezing Glodious's buttocks and rubs her back that is moving up and down. She rips off her bra and tears off her panties that was pulled to the side.

"Oh…shit…I love what you're packin', baby," moans Glodious.

"I'm about there, baby," says Jeff.

"Go ahead and let it erupt. Let your lava flow," moans Glodious. "Now!" she moans out even loudly.

He groans out as his lava fills into her female valley of pleasure. She screams as she reaches her climax. They both are exhausted as they lay naked in bed. They relax a few minutes after.

"I need to get up and go to the store. We need breakfast food," says Glodious.

"I can go get it, babe."

"No…I want to go. Give me a chance to be in the snow out there."

"Shit…you can have all the snow you want. I don't like the stuff," says Jeff as he pulls the sheet cover back over his naked body.

She gets up, and her naked body walks to the bedroom window. She peeks out from behind the blinds and curtains and stares at the white snow covering her neighborhood and their gray Chevy Impala.

Jeff stares at her naked body standing at the window. "Babe, will you bring back some Cheerios?"

"Cheerios? Nigga, please," says Glodious.

"So I like the little *Os*," says Jeff.

"The breakfast of champions," Glodious says, laughing.

"I ain't your champion?" asks Jeff.

She turns and stares at him lying half naked in bed. "Oh yeah… you're my champion, all right. You, well, hung, motherfucker."

They both laugh.

"Let me go get them Cheerios so I can keep you a champion in more ways than one," says Glodious.

They both laugh.

"Anything else?"

"I'll be right here when you get back."

She walks to her clothes on the floor, picks them up, and gets dressed.

*****

*Chicago Blizzard*

An hour later, the snow is coming down heavy and hard. The wind whirls it like small little tornadoes. Glodious is in her snow-covered car, driving back from the grocery store. Her windshield wipers are in full force, but she is still having a hard time seeing through the front windshield. A box of Cheerios sticks out of a full bag of groceries in the back seat. Glodious sees the traffic light is green just ahead. Because of the slick street, she drives slower and cautiously. Just as her car crosses into the middle of the intersection, a big rig truck rams the driver's side of her car. The car slides hundreds of yards on the snowy ice-covered street and flips over several times, coming to a dead stop, resting upside down. Glodious's body is halfway out of the driver's door window. She is out cold with blood dripping from her mouth and nose.

*****

Meanwhiles, it's dark, and a full moon illuminates the snow-covered graves and mausoleums in Oak Wood Cemetery. Ghosts are mingling about. Creadel is dressed in jeans, a rotten snow jacket, and dirty black shoes. He is sitting with his legs cross. Lil Candy is leaning against his headstone, giving herself a manicure. She is dressed in a black miniskirt, white blouse, black high heels, and a long, long white coat. She's chewing and popping gum; ever so often, she blows out a bubble gum and pops it.

"So when are we going to the West Side to see your sister, Creadel?"

"In a few hours."

"Why so late? Is it still a blizzard out there?" asks Lil Candy.

"You know snow doesn't affect us ghosts," says Creadel.

"Why?"

"You got something in mind?" asks Creadel.

"I just thought you and I would go down Joe's Juke Joint down there on Rest in Peace Boulevard in the graveyard club district. It's karaoke night," says Lil Candy.

"Karaoke?"

"Yeah," answers Lil Candy. "C'mon…let's have some fun… please…Creadel."

Creadel ponders. "Well, okay."

She plants a kiss on his jaw that leaves a red lipstick print.

"You didn't have to do that, woman."

"Yes…I did," says Lil Candy.

"All right, let's go to this karaoke thing," says Creadel.

They walk down the snow-covered graveyard until they come to the cross section road of Rest in Peace Boulevard and Stone Cold Drive in the cemetery.

In a large vacant section of Oak Wood Cemetery sits a large gray-stoned mausoleum isolated from the rest of the graves and mausoleums known as the social club district. The largest mausoleum sits with two large white Aphrodite, Greek goddess of love, bonded marble figurines. A neon sign over the door's entrance, flickering in red-and-green letterings, reads Joe's Juke Joint. The appearance of it is your regular-sized structured mausoleum that would only hold one deceased, but once inside, it's a full-scale-sized club with all the trimmings. The club's theme is that of the 1930's.

As Creadel and Lil Candy walk closer to Joe's Juke Joint, a few ghostly couple are seen entering it. One of the ghostly couples is grotesque in appearance with decades-old facial structures, and they are dressed in eighteenth-century attire with stains of blood on them. The other couple is from the 1920's, and they are dressed in that time period. They still look as if they are still young, just their skin are dead-gray.

Upon entering the club, Creadel and Lil Candy stand at the entrance, staring at the activities inside. The smoke fills the room from some of the smoking ghosts of various time periods. Ghosts are on the floor in front of a small platform where the DJ is setup doing a dance called steppin' to the DJ's stepper's music. Above the DJ's setup is a sign: Karaoke Night.

"There are a few seats over there," says Creadel.

"Okay."

He takes Lil Candy by her hand and takes her to a nearby round table and seat booth. Lil Candy slides into the booth and stares at the ghosts dancing. There are old tables and chairs with plaid black-and-white tablecloths. In the center of the tables are human skulls with a single lit candle inside. The club is dark inside. There's a long bar with a lime-green neon sign that reads Joe's Juke Joint behind it. Male ghosts are chatting the female ghosts who are dressed in sexy attire, some rotten, some not too worn out, sitting at the bar.

"Are you a stepper, Creadel?"

"I try…just can't get my feet to work with my mind of thought."

"Okay," replies Lil Candy. "Just watch how the guys are doing it on the dance floor."

"I'm checking it out," says Creadel.

A ghost waitress with stitches around her bald head and a long scar on her right jaw, dressed in a short waitress uniform, approaches their table. "Good evening, souls. My name is Duchess, and I'm your waitress for the night. What can I get you for starters?"

Creadel looks at Lil Candy.

"Um…whatcha got?" asks Lil Candy.

"Baby, we can make you whatever your little heart desires."

"Um…okay." She looks into Creadel's eyes. "I'll have a French Kiss."

"Okay…one French Kiss with a lemon twist and strain…correct?" says the waitress.

"Yes."

"How about you, sir?"

"Give me a shot of Old Grand-Dad."

"Coming right up."

The waitress leaves.

Lil Candy pulls a pack of cigarettes from her small purse and lights one with a Bic lighter. "So you really want to go to your half sista and confront her about something she and your half brother did in the past?"

"She has carried all this hatred of my mother far too…long. I have to set this shit straight," says Creadel.

"Well…if you must."

"I must, believe me, I must," says Creadel.

*****

It's still heavily snowing outside the hospital. An ambulance with lights flashing and siren going pulls into the emergency entrance. The paramedics pull an injured woman and rush her inside. Glodious's husband, Jeff, is getting off the hospital's elevator on the third floor. With flowers in hand, he walks to Glodious's room where she lies in a coma. He stands inside her room, looking at the monitoring equipment connected to her, the IV line in her left arm, the white linen she's covered with, and the bandage wrapped around her head. He walks to her bedside, leans down, and kisses her on the lips.

"I love you, baby."

Because she's in a coma, she cannot respond.

# CHAPTER 10

Back at the cemetery's ghost joint, the DJ has stopped playing his music. The dance floor is empty. A few customers are mingling about, having drinks and conversations, while the DJ is on a break.

After returning from the ladies' room, Lil Candy slides her way into their booth next to Creadel. Creadel is a little drunk as he stares at Lil Candy's short skirt rising up her thighs as she slides into their booth next to him. She notices. She's a little tipsy as well. Several empty glasses sit on their table beside an ashtray full of cigarette butts with red lipstick prints on them.

"Um…feelin'…good…as all…hell," says drunk Lil Candy.

"Damn…Candy. I must say, girl, you got some fine-ass legs."

"Whatcha sayin', Creadel? You feelin' a little horny, are you? You want to play house or somethin' maybe?"

Creadel looks at her thighs, then her breasts, then her lips. He starts to speak but is interrupted by the DJ speaking into his microphone.

"Okay! Folks! It's time for our annual karaoke!" the DJ yells out.

"Yay!" Lil Candy yells out. "We gonna do karaoke?" asks Lil Candy.

"Woman, I don't do karaoke 'cause I don't do karaoke."

"Oh, please, Creadel…do it for Lil Candy. You can sing, can't you?"

"Baby, I can sing like James Brown…I…I…I…can sing," says Creadel. "I can sing like anybody if I want to."

"Well, okay, we're gonna do it then," replies Lil Candy.

"Naw…we ain't. I ain't ready to be laughed at tonight," says Creadel.

"C'mon, boo…stop being a party pooper."

The DJ starts playing music for a female transparent ghost Erica Pelosi, who's in her thirties. She is Caucasian, nicely shaped and tall, wearing a white dress with a red rose on the right upper side of her shoulder dress. Her hair is long and curly and blond. Her lipstick matches the color of her red rose. Erica walks to the DJ and whispers into his ear. He hands her the microphone. She walks and stands in front of the small platform in front of the DJ's setup. The DJ starts playing the music to "God Bless the Child" by Billie Holiday. The room goes pitch-black. Suddenly, a spotlight hit Erica's whole body standing at the microphone. She starts singing "God Bless the Child."

"That's got his own!"

The ghost audience goes crazy and applauds because she sounds so good.

"Good grief…not another 'God Bless the Child' song," says Creadel.

"Oh! Hell naw!" yells out Lil Candy. "She ain't all that!" says Lil Candy.

"I…don't know, Candy. She is nailing it, though," says Creadel.

Lil Candy gives Creadel an evil eye and shrugs her shoulders. Erica ends her song, and the crowd applauds as she walks to her seat at the bar.

Another contender walks to the DJ; this time, it's a male ghost named Leo. Leo is tall with dark complexion, has decomposed skin, is in his thirties, and has a small Afro with a streak of gray on the left side. He is dressed in a white dirty shirt with a bloodstain in the center where the heart is. His black pants have holes at the knees, and his shoes are dirty. He also has a scar around his neck.

Leo whispers into the DJ's ear and walks in front of the DJ's setup. The room goes pitch-black again. Only the lighted ends of cigarettes can be seen. Suddenly, Leo's loud voice sings out the song "A Heart Is a House for Love." A loud and long *O* comes out of Leo's mouth as he starts singing. The spotlight hits him in the face.

As Leo sings, the female ghosts are fanning their faces to keep from fainting and patting their chests. Lil Candy is fanning her face. "Damn…that brotha can sing," says Lil Candy.

"He all right, nothin' big," says Creadel.

Lil Candy gives him a look of "Really?"

"Can you do better?" asks Lil Candy.

Creadel ponders a little. "Hmm…maybe."

As Leo sings, Creadel gets up and walks to the DJ's setup. With his finger, Creadel beckons the DJ to come closer to him. The DJ comes to Creadel and leans down so Creadel can talk to him. Creadel tells him something. The DJ acknowledges by shaking his head. Lil Candy looks puzzled as she stares at them. Creadel walks to the side of the DJ's setup. He beckons for Lil Candy to come. She walks to him; Creadel whispers into her ear. She says "okay," and they wait for Leo to finish singing. Leo ends his song and walks away as two pairs of panties are thrown at him. All applaud him.

The DJ starts playing the instrumental version of CeeLo Green's "Closet Freak." Creadel grabs the two microphones and hands one to Lil Candy. Lil Candy starts. The crowd doesn't realize what's going on until Lil Candy starts singing her part of "Closet Freak" as she walks from out in front of the crowd. She starts dancing as Creadel starts singing "Closet Freak." The Ghost Joint goes wild and crazy to them singing and performing. Several attractive young female ghosts join in on the floor and dance to their performance. They are dressed in short skirts and shorts with red, green, and black houses and wearing white go-go boots. They all are wearing big Afro's, white, black, and lime-green. Moments later, the whole club is on the floor, dancing to Creadel and Lil Candy singing "Closet Freak."

*****

Meanwhile, outside Mercy Hospital on the near southside, it's windy and snowy as the blizzard over the city is continuing. Glodious's husband, Jeff, is wearing a thick overcoat with snow on the shoulders, a head cap with earflaps that covers his ears, a long winter scarf wrapped around his neck, a heavy sweater, and a pair of blue jeans with the legs of them stuffed inside his snow boots. Jeff stumps through the deep snow.

Jeff's heavy thick snow gloved-covered hands are carrying a bouquet of flowers for Glodious. A man is shoveling snow from around his car. An ambulance with siren and flashing lights makes its way to the hospital's emergency entrance. Jeff enters the hospital's entrance. He walks to the elevator and presses the button. He enters and presses the third-floor button. The door closes.

The third floor of the hospital is a little busy with nurses moving about, doing their routine duties. A few doctors are assisting patients. An elderly man in his hospital gown, sitting in a wheelchair with bandages wrapped around his head, sits patiently next to the receptionist's desk. Glodious is lying in her bed, still in a coma, as Jeff enters. He stands at the door and just stares at his wife's body covered in white linen, with IVs connected to her arms. A heart monitor connected to her shows her heart beat. He walks to her and kisses her. He places the flowers in a vase sitting on the long square heater at the window that overlooks the expressway in front of the hospital. He stares out for a moment. He pulls the chair next to her bed and sits down. A tear slowly runs down the side of his nose. He sits patiently, holding her hand.

*****

In the wee hours of the night, Creadel and Lil Candy are walking back through the cemetery to their graves.

"Shit, I hate snow. Too much of it and it's cold as hell out here," says Lil Candy.

"I know, but we are ghosts. We can deal with anything," says Creadel.

"Man…you surprised me. I didn't know you could sing like the bro Ceelo Green, Creadel, and you were dancin'. Kinda got me all hot and bothered."

"Yeah, well…I got a few skills. Don't worry, Lil Candy, the snow will cool you off."

"I don't need snow. I need a man." She stops in her tracks and puts her hands on her hips. "What's the matter? You need a couple of Viagras?"

"What Viagra! Woman, please, I have you know I don't need no Viagra for nothin'," says Creadel, pouting.

"Real…ly," says Lil Candy.

"Really," answers Creadel.

"*Prove it!*"

"I ain't *gotta*…prove a darn thing. I'm as good as it gets, even better."

"Prove it then to Lil Candy."

"Look, I'm on a mission," says Creadel.

"You mean you're on a mission. I just wanna play house the old…fashioned…way," says Lil Candy. "Can you *rise*…to the occasion?" asks Lil Candy.

"Wouldn't you like to know?"

"Why, yes…I really, really would," says Lil Candy.

"Let's focus on my mission at hand and go to my half sister's place. Can we do that?"

"I guess."

"Here's your plot. I'll come get you when I'm ready to leave, so be ready."

"Okay, I will."

Lil Candy stands atop her grave and dissolves into it. Creadel walks through the snow-covered graveyard to his grave and dissolves into it.

# CHAPTER 11

A few days later, Creadel and Lil Candy are standing outside Creadel's half sister's home on the southside of Chicago. The neighborhood is quiet, no one outside except for a few neighbors shoveling snow and wiping snow off their cars and walkways.

"Okay, now what, Creadel?"

"Well, we go in and confront her about what she did to my mother."

"You think she's gonna start talkin' and tellin' you?" asks Lil Candy.

The both of them walk through the front of the house structure.

Inside the house is quiet except for the TV sitting in the living room that has a snowy screen because there's no signal. The living room is furnished with contemporary furniture and large artificial green plants. Jeff (Glodious's husband) is sitting on the sofa, looking depressed as he watches an episode of *Graveyard Society.* The first episode is about a graveyard digger brutally murdered and is given seventy-two hours to avenge his untimely demise. Creadel and Lil Candy are standing at the living room's front door, staring at Jeff sitting on the sofa. Being ghosts, he can't see them.

In front of the sofa is a contemporary coffee table with his cell phone lying next to an ashtray with marijuana butts and cigarette butts in it. An empty can of Old Style beer sits a few inches away from the ashtray.

Creadel is looking around for Glodious.

"Where is Glodious?"

"I don't know."

"Let's look in the other rooms of the house," says Creadel.

They search all the rooms of the house. Still no Glodious to be seen. They go back into the living room and watch Jeff.

"Well, she ain't here," says Lil Candy.

"That's a fact," replies Creadel. "I guess we just wait a minute. Maybe she'll come back from where she is," says Creadel.

"Old boy there is kinda cute," says Lil Candy.

"I'm not into men, Candy. Shit."

"I've been tryin' to give you all of me, all…of me, and you just keep refusing my goodness. You know what? Since you don't wanna give Candy no satisfaction…I'll just have to at least have some fun with old Jeffy here," says Lil Candy.

Jeff has dosed off to sleep on the sofa.

"What are you thinking, Candy?"

"I ain't thinkin' about nothin', just gonna have me a little fun."

Creadel walks to a nearby dark-brown leather high-back chair in the corner of the living room and sits. Lil Candy walks to the sofa where Jeff is asleep. She gently rubs his head. Jeff shifts from his side to lying on his back. Lil Candy stares at his red shirt with white buttons on his chest. She notices his black hairy chest. Jeff is snoring. She slowly walks to the side of the sofa and leans down close to his chest and lightly rubs his chest hair. He quickly opens his eyes. Not seeing anything, he falls back to sleep.

"Lil Candy! What the hell are you doing, woman?"

"Mind your business, Creadel. You had your chance," says Lil Candy. Lil Candy stares at Jeff's pants. She stares at the zipper. She slowly and gently unzips his pants. She slowly slides her right hand inside his pants. She starts feeling his groin. "Damn, this hunk of beef feels so nice," says Lil Candy.

Jeff, in shock, wakes up quickly, looking around and at his unzipped pants.

"Shit, just when I was about to mess with his pecker," says Lil Candy.

Jeff sees no one in the room. "Damn, musta had a wet dream," he says to himself. His cell phone rings. Jeff answers his phone.

"Hello. Oh, hi, Janice. I was there last night, and she is still in a coma. The doctors say she was lucky to be alive. Yeah. She's at Mercy

Hospital on the third floor," he tells her. "Yeah. Okay. Thanks, I'll let you know if anything changes. Okay, bye."

"You hear that, Creadel? Your sister's in a coma, Creadel."

"Okay, c'mon, we gotta go," says Creadel.

"Where are we going, Creadel?"

"To the hospital."

"In the cold?"

"Don't worry, you're a ghost. You can't feel nothin'."

"Well, how are we gonna get there?" asks Lil Candy.

"Same way we got here. We're gonna ride…the winds."

"Can't we just go like ordinary people?"

"But we ain't ordinary," says Creadel. "We are ghosts or have you forgotten that?"

"The thought has never left my mind," says Lil Candy.

"Good, let's go."

*Later that same night*

Glodious's hospital room is quiet; only the sound of her heart monitor and other equipment connected to her are heard as she lies in bed, still in a coma. A nurse—heavyset African American woman in her thirties, dark complexion, long hair in a ponytail, and wearing her nurse uniform—enters the room and checks her vitals. She sticks a thermometer in Glodious's mouth and checks her pulse. The nurse walks to the end of Glodious's bed and writes Glodious's vitals on a clipboard and leaves the room.

The wall on the left side of the room is a simple plain white wall with nothing on it. Slowly, a glowing grayish cloud forming in the center of it comes into play with electric surge sparking inside it. The nurse can't see it. The ceiling lights in the bedroom start flickering off and on. Suddenly, Creadel and Lil Candy emerge from within the center of the cloud forming a space in Glodious's hospital room. The two of them stand, looking at Glodious lying in her bed.

"Okay. What now?" asks Lil Candy.

"Well, we just have to wait and see if she recovers," says Creadel.

"What! That could take hours, days, months, even years, and maybe never," says Lil Candy.

"I know," replies Creadel.

"Hell…I know we're ghosts, but even ghosts have little patience when it comes to waitin'," says Lil Candy.

"I know. I know. Let's think a minute here on what we can do or what choices we have, okay, Lil Candy?"

"Yeah, okay," answers Lil Candy.

The two of them are very quiet as they think.

Moments later, Lil Candy yells, "I got it!"

"What?" asks Creadel.

"She's in a coma, right?"

"Yeah," answers Creadel.

"Well, why don't we go over her and beat her ass for whatever it was she did to your mama?" says Lil Candy.

"We can't do that, Candy!"

"Why not?"

"She's comatose," says Creadel.

"She ain't gonna feel a damn…thing," says Lil Candy.

"That would be inhuman for ghosts to do," says Creadel.

"So?" replies Lil Candy.

"Gotta be a better way," says Creadel.

They both start pondering in their thoughts again.

"What she did to your mother was so unforgettable, right, Creadel? Damn…skippy…why don't we go over there and accidently tip over her bed, and her ass would be on this cold-ass floor in pain. Maybe that would wake her ass up out of the coma," says Lil Candy.

"Woman…you have devious mind."

"What's devious?" asks Lil Candy.

"Never mind, don't worry about it."

They think for a few more minutes.

"You know, Candy, she's in this coma state, right?"

"Yeah."

"And we do have certain powers, right?" says Creadel.

"Yep, foe sho," says Lil Candy. "What you got in mind, Creadel?"

"Umm…thinkin' that maybe…just maybe…we can borrow her soul. I mean, she's just like being dead…right? Let's take her soul on a learning experience."

Lil Candy ponders a moment. "Yeah…we can definitely get her soul, being that it's like being dead anyway," says Candy, laughing. "Okay, so we get her comatose soul and do what with it, Creadel?"

"Well, we take it to one of our fellow ghosts for a little mind readjustment," says Creadel.

"Sounds like a plan to me," says Lil Candy.

"Okay, let's do it," says Creadel.

"It's on…now, baby!" Lil Candy cries out.

They walk to the side of Glodious's bed. Creadel stares down at her. Creadel starts performing some sort of voodoo ritual over Glodious's body with his hands, saying some words in Arabic that even Lil Candy doesn't understand. She looks puzzled as hell at Creadel waving his hands over Glodious's body and trying to speak in Arabic, then in English.

"Come…come…Glodious…rise. I beckon you to rise your soul, Glodious," says Creadel.

"Rise, bitch," says Lil Candy.

"Calmness, Candy. Calmness, all right?" says Creadel.

Nothing's happening at the moment. Lil Candy walks to the end of the bed and kicks it. Slowly, the soul of Glodious rises from inside her body.

"Aw…here you are," says Creadel.

Glodious looks around the room, confused, and at Creadel. "What are you doing here, Creadel? Where am I? What's going on? Am I dead?" asks Glodious.

"Well…yes and no," says Creadel. "I guess something happened to you, and you ended up here in the hospital," says Creadel.

"But you are dead, Creadel. I was at your funeral."

"You mean…we are dead," interrupts Lil Candy.

"I heard what you said standing over my body at my funeral there."

"You did?"

"Hell yeah," says Creadel.

"So we are all ghosts now?"

"You bet your bottom shorts, darlin'," says Lil Candy.

"Creadel, who's this woman?" asks Glodious.

"She's my friend from beyond."

"From beyond? From beyond what?"

"The other side," says Lil Candy.

"I'm a ghost?"

"No…we are all ghosts, sorta," says Creadel.

"Oh shit!" says Glodious. "I'm dead?"

"Well…sorta…a little bit of yes…and a little bit of no… depends on how you look at it," says Lil Candy.

"Why are you here?"

"Well, little sis, we need to clear up a few things of what you did in your conscious state of mind when Mom was among the living," Creadel tells her.

"You do…remember his mom…don't cha?" asks Lil Candy.

"Of course, I remember her. Where are you going with this?" asks Glodious.

"You see, that's the thing here, sis. We are going to take you on a little trip with us."

"What if I don't wanna go?" says Glodious.

"Oh…you're goin'. You ain't got no…freakin' choice, chicky," says Lil Candy.

"Don't worry, we'll have you back here in no time," says Creadel. "So just take my arm, and off we go," says Creadel.

Glodious nervously takes Creadel's right arm, and they all walk back through the cloud-formed open space in the wall and disappear.

# CHAPTER 12

A few hours later, the three of them are back in Oak Wood Cemetery. The snow has stopped, and there's a lot of ghost activity. Ghost kids are playing about in the graveyard. At one mausoleum, a transparent female ghost is dressed in a white rotten long gown. Her long white hair is blowing in the wind as she sits in her white rocking chair, crocheting. At another mausoleum, three transparent rapper in their teens—one African American, one Caucasian, and one Filipino—are all singing to some rap music from the transparent boombox sitting by them on the ground. A transparent ghost prisoner in his fifties, dressed in his striped red-and-white prison uniform, is seen running and being chased by two transparent police ghosts who are in hot pursuit.

"What the hell is this place?" asks Glodious.

"This is the other side…Glodious," says Creadel.

"The place they call the beyond," replies Lil Candy.

"There's even a courthouse and other businesses here? Can we be seen?" asks Glodious.

"Yes, but ghosts can only be seen by other ghosts, not humans," says Creadel.

"Unless the ghosts want to be seen," adds Lil Candy.

"This is one freakin' ghostly experience I'm having," says Glodious.

"This is where your soul rests until it makes its final transition," says Creadel.

"Really?"

"Yes," says Creadel.

"So why am I here, Creadel?"

"Because you have been carrying some very bad knowledge and screwed-up feelings about my mom, the woman you tried to murder. I decided to let you know exactly what happened when we were kids. But first, I have to see if I can apply for permission to see your life digitally at This Was Your Life Studio."

Looking puzzled, Glodious asks, "This Was Your Life Studio?"

"Yeah, girlfriend," replies Lil Candy.

"You'll see," says Creadel. "Come on, Glodious, we have to go there now. It's just down there on Graveyard Boulevard," Creadel tells her.

Looking inquisitive, her transparent body follows them down the asphalt paved road to the studio.

*Minutes later*

Outside the studio is quiet and dark. There's a full moon as clouds pass underneath it. Two possums roam about the graveyard, searching for food. Their eyes glow from the moonlight. Creadel, Lil Candy, and Glodious are standing in front This Was Your Life Studio entrance.

"Okay, here we are," says Creadel.

"Well, knock on the door, dude," says Lil Candy.

"All right! All right! Give me a minute already," says Creadel. He finally knock three times on the gray steel gothic-looking door, stands back, and waits.

From behind the gray steel door, yells out hostess Nikki Barber, "Who is it?"

"It's me, Creadel, Nikki!"

"What do you want this time of the night?" yells out hostess Nikki. "I'm trying to rest in peace!" says Nikki.

"Sorry to disturb you! I just want to apply for a permit to show someone who needs to be shown what she did in her life to my mother when we were young. It's a matter of great urgency!" yells out Creadel.

"She's a comatose soul!" yells out Lil Candy.

"Comatose soul?" asks Nikki.

Both Creadel and Lil Candy say yes at the same time. Glodious looks at them, puzzled.

"I'm comatose?" asks Glodious.

The door slowly opens. The hostess sticks her head out the door, showing her hair rolled up in large rollers, wearing a long rotten, dirty cotton sleeping gown. Her face is caked with an overdose of facial cream.

"Come on in," says Nikki.

The three of them enter the mausoleum, which is now a huge room with a coffin and an old dirty dresser with cobwebs on it. Creadel, Lil Candy, and Glodious are standing in front of hostess Nikki.

"What can I do for you all?" asks Nikki.

"Well, my sister needs to see what was her life like back then, especially about the time when our Pop took her and her brother from their mother," says Creadel.

Nikki looks at Glodious. "So is this your sister, the comatose one?"

"Yes," replies Creadel.

"Well, she needs to fill out an application to see if it gets approved," says Nikki.

"Okay, fine, let's get the ball rolling," says Creadel.

"Okay." Nikki walks to her sleeping section of the studio to a nightstand and pulls out an application and an ink pen. She hands it to Glodious. "Fill this out."

Glodious fills out the application quickly and hands it back to hostess Nikki. The hostess walks the application to a processing machine, turns it on, and inserts the application and waits for a respond on the monitor screen. She types in the information. They wait patiently. Creadel paces back and forth. Lil Candy is standing with her arms crossed and her right feet tapping the floor. Glodious just stands staring around the studio. Hostess Nikki is standing at the machine, staring at the screen.

After a few minutes, the results appear on the screen in dripping-red bloody letters: denied!

"Oh…well…we tried," says hostess Nikki. "Comatose one here must have did something in her past that was despicable," says hostess Nikki.

"What did I do?" asks Glodious.

"You don't remember?" asks Lil Candy.

"No. I don't."

"Little sista, looks like I have to do this myself. Come over here and take a seat," says Creadel.

They walk to a few director's chairs across the room on the set, and only Lil Candy, Glodious, and hostess Nikki sit in them. Creadel stands in front of them. He starts pacing back and forth, rubbing his chin.

# CHAPTER 13

"You, Glodious, came to my funeral. You stood over my casket, looking down at my dead body. You started thinking in your mind how much you hated me and my mother, the woman who raised you and your brother while your dad was out fucking around on her."

"You read…my mind?"

Creadel giggles.

"You thought that being dead, the soul can't hear your thoughts? Baby, not only can we hear your thoughts we can also do lots of stuff you can't even imagine us ghosts can do," says Lil Candy.

"Yeah, I heard everything you said to me lying stiff as a doornail in my coffin. After all these years…growing up with you and your brother, I didn't realize how much you really hated me and my mom. Why?" asks Creadel.

Pouting, she answers, "Your mother took us from my mother!" yells out Glodious. "And you said that you didn't want us living with you! I remember you saying it!" yells out Glodious.

Still pacing, Creadel says, "I remember that, Glodious. I was so young back then, Glodious. I didn't know what I was saying! I was a little kid myself. So that's what you think you know. Shit! I need to smoke me a joint."

"You want a joint?" asks hostess Nikki.

"Anything will do!" replies Creadel.

Hostess Nikki pulls out a ready-made joint and Bic lighter from her bosom. She lights it, inhales, blows out the smoke, and hands it to Creadel, who does the same thing.

"Don't forget I'm next, Creadel," says Lil Candy.

He hands it to Lil Candy. "Okay, where was I? Oh yeah. Glodious, you are dead. Ooops, shouldn't use that word. You are wrong. Let me tell you, Glodious, what went down back then.

"I remember that night so clearly back then when we were kids. It was very cold that night, so cold you could see your breath as you breathe out. It was me, I was about seven or eight at the time, Pops and another man, can't remember who he was, could have been one of our uncles or maybe just a friend. We walked a long way in the cold of winter to an alley. Pop kicked open the wooden backyard fence gate, which led to the back of a house. We went to an outside door of a bedroom. Dad kicked open the door. We entered, and man, that room was so hot from the heater. There was about four very young kids lying in bed, asleep. Dad grabbed a sheet and wrapped it around you. The other man grabbed your brother and did the same. There was no other adult in the room. We quickly left out the way we entered. You, Glodious, my mother didn't take you from your mother like you think. That was your dad's doing. Why he did it? We will never know. Maybe he saw something that your mother was doing wrong with you and your brother?

"After that, your daddy…brought you and your brother to my mom and asked her to help him raise you, which she reluctantly did because she loved him. And you said that I didn't want you all to live with us. Glodious…you have to understand…back then, I was just a kid myself. I didn't mean it. Any kid would feel that. Having some kids invade their world is scary to a kid. For that, I apologize. But we grew up. I loved both of you even though Pops still played around on my mother as she did her best to raise you both. And the both of you gave her hell for it."

"She's responsible for what happened!" yells out Glodious.

"How the hell you figure that shit, Glodious? Dad took the both of you. My mom didn't even know what he was doing until he brought you to her. She didn't even know that you existed!" yells out Creadel. "Woman, you should have been thankin' her for puttin' up with another woman's illegitimate kids. I sure as hell wouldn't have done it!" yells out Lil Candy.

"So all these years you've been holding this grudge…and hatred. But at least your brother apologized to my mom before she died, and I was grateful for that, Glodious."

"That's what happened?" asks Glodious.

"Yes," replies Creadel. "Even when we were grown, you would come to my house parties and everything, not showing that you really didn't like me. It was all an act of fakeness. You were a two-faced sister, girl. I thought you did. You broke my heart, sis. And you did the unthinkable…you tried to do bodily harm or even kill my mother by putting pieces of broken glass in her plate."

"She did that to your mother, Creadel?" asks Lil Candy.

"Yeah."

"You want me to kick her ass for you, Creadel?"

"Naw, God will deal with her."

"Shit…maybe God is punishing her already. She's comatose, ain't she? That's the same as being dead, ain't it?" says hostess Nikki.

"Wow, I didn't realize what I did," says Glodious. "So how can I make it right?" ask Glodious.

"Not sure if you can, Glodious," says Creadel.

"There must be something I can do."

"Why don't you start by apologizing, comatose?" says hostess Nikki.

"Creadel, your mother had a good heart. Not many women would have done what she did. I give her props," says Lil Candy.

"Thanks, Lil Candy."

"Girlfriend…if I was you…I would go to his mom's grave and ask for forgiveness because God knows all. He just might not let you wake up from your comatose state or you just might end up staying with us on a permanent basis," says Lil Candy.

"Wow, I've been wrong all these years. I'm so sorry, Creadel, for the damage I've caused to you and your mother."

"When, if, you recover from this comatose state, you should go to your mother and ask her why Pops took you and your brother that night and why it took all these years to when you were grown and she didn't try to get you both back."

"Yeah, I'll do just that, Creadel." Teary-eyed, she hugged Creadel. "You know, if I don't wake up from this, being here, it's not so bad."

They all giggle.

"Okay, just walk down this path to the cemetery's steel gates, and once you step out, you will be back to where you were in real life," says Creadel.

# CHAPTER 14

The cemetery is illuminated from the full moon. Ghosts are among the graves and mausoleums, doing various activities. Creadel and Lil Candy are sitting on a bench with cobwebs on its rear bench leg. They are watching the activities of ghosts in the cemetery.

"You know, Lil Candy, I feel good now that I set Glodious on the truth to what happened to her and her brother."

"Yeah, you did a good thing, Creadel. Your mother would be proud of you."

"You think?"

"Yes, you spoke up for your mother, man. I'm proud of you, dude."

"Damn, baby, you're making me fill a little blushy."

"I can do more if you want me to."

About three hundred feet from them, a transparent Caucasian female ghost in her forties, dressed in flowing white dress and white high heels, comes from within her mausoleum, carrying an old square wooden record player. Her face is pale and beautiful with long snow-white hair as she sits the record player on the ground in front of her mausoleum's entrance. She pulls out a rocking chair with a record album on the seat. She places the rocking chair next to the record player and sits. She puts the transparent album on her lap. Creadel and Lil Candy notice her.

She takes her finger and give the turntable a good spin. She pulls out the album and places it on the spinning turntable and places the needle on it. Creadel starts singing Teddy Pendergrass's "Come Go with Me." Lil Candy starts to move to the music in her seat. Creadel stands up in front of Lil Candy with his hand out to her. Lil Candy is stunned. Creadel starts singing the words of the song to Lil Candy as he pulls her up to slow dance. Lil Candy is in awe.

Creadel starts singing. "Come go with me," sings Creadel. "Come on over to my place…I don't feel like being lonely tonight. You see, I need some company…And you look like you're just my type," sings Creadel.

"Really?" replies Lil Candy, blushing.

Creadel continues singing to Lil Candy.

"And now…you wanna play house to some Teddy Pendergrass?" Creadel nods.

"Oh…Jesus. Thank you, Lord," says Lil Candy.

The music continues to play as they walk arm in arm down the illuminating asphalt paved road to Creadel's grave.

"I guess I can rest in peace now," says Creadel.

"Yes you can," says Lil Candy.

The graveyard goes to pitch-black darkness.

*Few weeks later*

On a sunny afternoon in Oak Wood Cemetery, a pair of nicely shaped woman's legs wearing stockings and a pair of black high heels are seen walking through the graveyard and stops at a headstone that reads

> Beloved wife and mother
> Marie J.
> 1934–1985

Glodious, standing over the grave, places flowers at the base of the headstone. "I came to apologize, Marie, for the way me and my brother treated you. I'm so very sorry." Glodious kneels down to the grave and places her hand on it. "I'm asking for your forgiveness."

Without notice, a pair of transparent skeletal arms and hands burst from beneath the grave and grab Glodious by her neck and pull her deep inside the grave.

Glodious wakes up from her coma with Jeff's hand holding hers as he is sleeping with his head laying by her bedside. She has the look of being afraid—very afraid.

*****

Now at Oak Wood Cemetery, it's night. The graveyard is quiet. No ghosts is present at all. Off in the distance, a mausoleum has the lime-green neon sign over the door entrance that reads:

The GRIP
Ghost Rest in Peace
Radio Station

It's the only ghost radio station in Oak Wood Cemetery's graveyard society. Inside, the mausoleum is set up like a real radio station. The DJ is a female ghost, is in her thirties, has long blond hair, has skeletal-looking body and face, and has dead-gray decomposed skin. Her eyes are sunken. Her lips are painted with red lipstick. She wears a baseball cap and T-shirt with a large gold chain around her neck. She sits at her desk and speaks into the microphone.

"Good evening to all my fellow ghosts here in Oak Wood Cemetery! You're listening to G-R-I-P radio. I'm your ghostist…with the mostist. So all rise! It's time for all you spooks to get your groove on! This one is for all of you stepper ghosts out there."

The DJ starts playing "Cleo's Mood/Cleo's Back" by Jr. Walker & All the Stars. Ghosts start rising from their graves and start dancing. Oak Wood Cemetery comes alive in the graveyard society.

The End

*Many thanks to my readers. Here is something extra for you.*

What I'm about to tell you really happened.

It wasn't a figment of my imagination at all.

It happened one day last summer, on a sunny morning. I was in my house office doing something. I went into the kitchen. I started to place a dish in the kitchen sink to rinse off. But something caught my attention outside on the side of my house. I looked out the kitchen window, which had blinds open. There was this black shiny oblong object whirling around on the ground. At first, I thought it was a black plastic bag in the wind. There was no wind, and the leaves on the palm tree were not moving. I stared at it for about twenty seconds, watching it whirl and take a few bounces. The black object had no presence of anything of life—no head, no eyes no tail, no feet, no body. I was so puzzled. *What the hell is that?* I thought to myself. Then as it kept whirling around without stopping, out came a black cat. "What the fuck?" I said out loud. I was startled.

I kept my eyes on it as the black cat slowly strolled to the brick wall that separated my house and my neighbor's yard. The cat just jumped on the brick wall on the side of my house and left. I was so glad the cat didn't see me inside standing at the kitchen window, staring at it.

I know this sounds crazy. I couldn't believe what I saw myself. But as God is my witness, this actually happened. So now on I really look at cats in a different way.

From time to time, I still see that cat in my backyard or in the neighborhood.

# ABOUT THE AUTHOR

Everett D. Wair Sr. is a retired Amtrak employee. He lives in California with his beautiful wife, Rosemarie L. Wair, and his beloved dog, Dexter. He is a proud father of three fantastic sons: Melvin C. Wair, Marcus Wair, and Everett Wair Jr. He is a published writer of *Graveyard Society*, *Playing a Dangerous Game*, and the soon-to-be-released *Graveyard Society: Eve*. He hopes that one of his fantastic books will make it onto the silver screen. He welcomes any and all production companies and producers to contact Page Publishing for contact information.